PIANO / VOCAL / GUITAR

CASTING CROWNS
COME TO THE WELL

ISBN 978-1-4584-1655-1

HAL•LEONARD®
CORPORATION
7777 W. BLUEMOUND RD. P.O. BOX 13819 MILWAUKEE, WI 53213

Visit Hal Leonard Online at
www.halleonard.com

COURAGEOUS

Words and Music by MARK HALL
and MATTHEW WEST

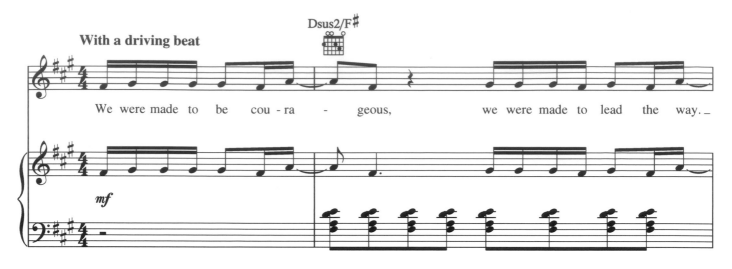

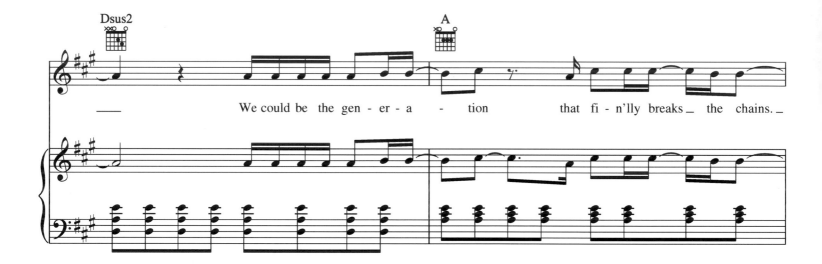

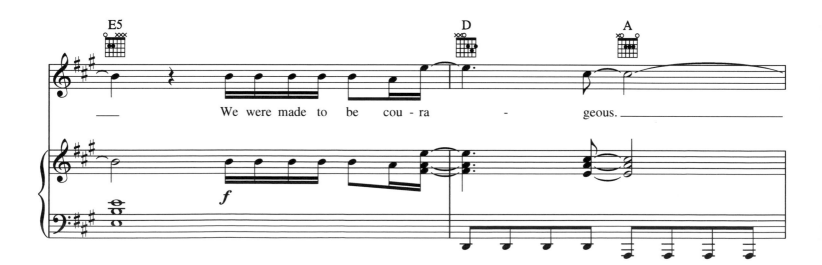

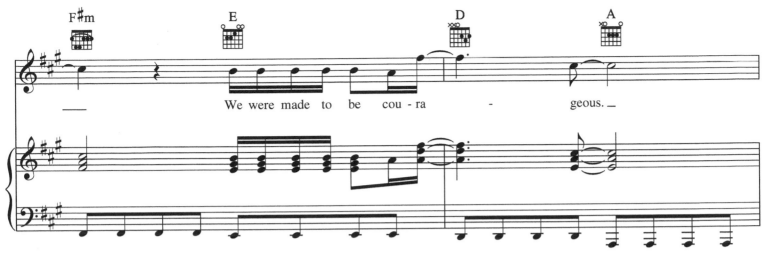

We were made to be cou - ra - geous. __

We were war - riors on __ the front __ lines, stand - ing un - a - fraid, __

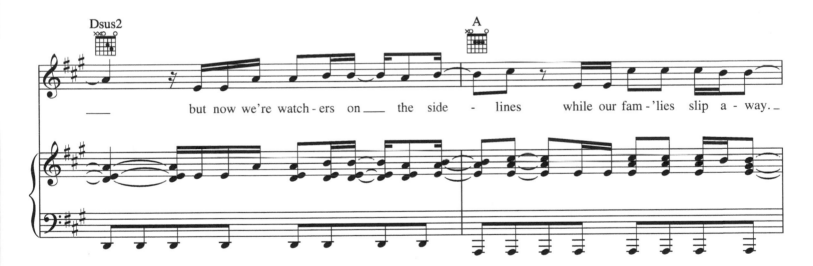

__ but now we're watch - ers on __ the side - lines while our fam - 'lies slip a - way. __

__ Where are you, men of cour - age? You were made for so __ much more. __

Let the pound-ing of our hearts ___ cry, "We will serve ___ the Lord!" ___

We were made to be cou-ra-geous, and we're tak-ing back ___ the fight. ___

We were made to be cou-ra-geous, and it starts with us ___ to-night. ___

The on-ly way ___ we'll ev-er stand ___ is on our knees ___

with lift - ed hands.__ Make us cou - ra - - geous._____

Lord, make us cou - ra - geous._____ This is our res-o-lu-

- tion, our an - swer to the call.__ We will love our wives__ and chil-

- dren; we re - fuse to let__ them fall.__ We will re - ig - nite__ the pas-

-sion   that we bur-ied deep_ in-side.___   May the watch-ers be - come war-

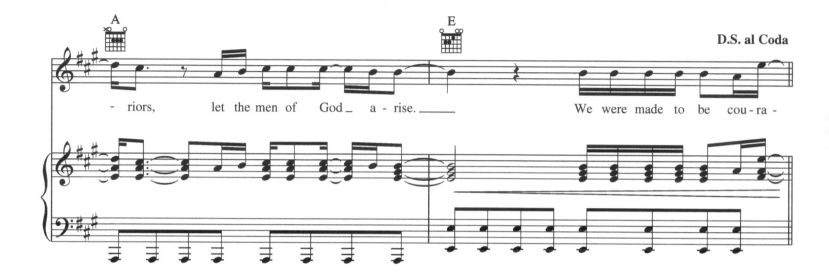

D.S. al Coda

-riors,   let the men of God_ a-rise.___   We were made to be cou-ra-

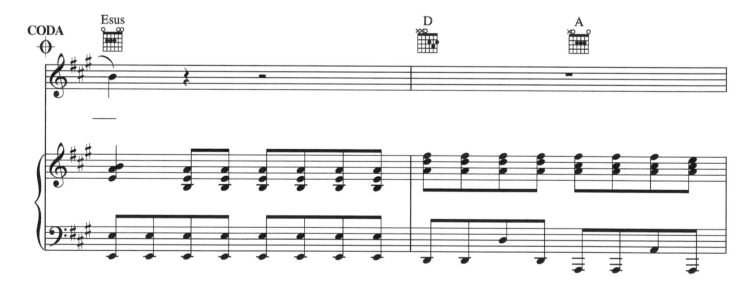

CODA

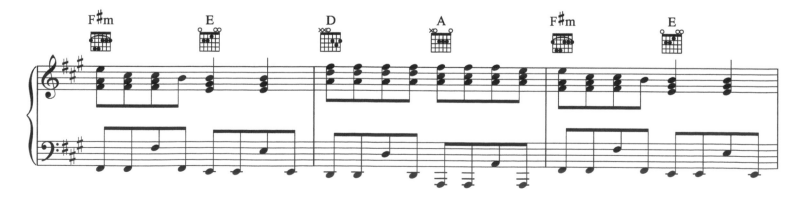

Seek jus - tice, love mer - cy, ___ walk hum - bly with your ___ God.

Seek jus - tice, love mer - cy, ___ walk hum - bly with your ___ God. In the war ___

___ of the mind, ___ I will make ___ my stand, in the bat - tle of the heart ___ and the bat -

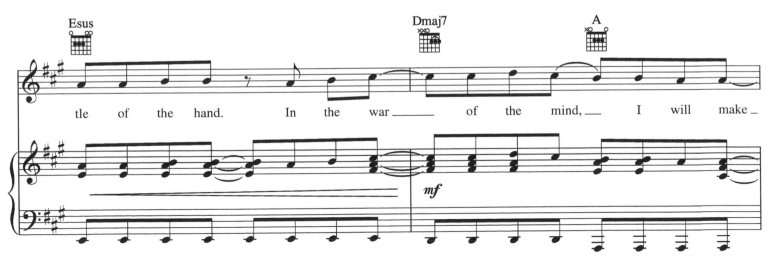

tle of the hand. In the war _____ of the mind, ___ I will make ___

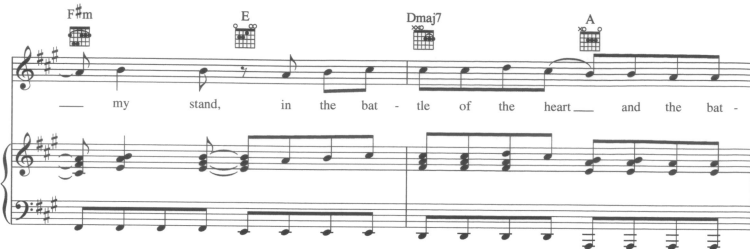

— my stand, in the bat - tle of the heart___ and the bat -

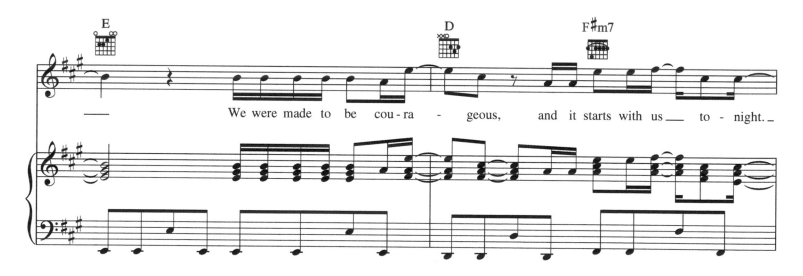

tle of the hand. We were made to be cou - ra - geous, and we're tak - ing back___ the fight.___

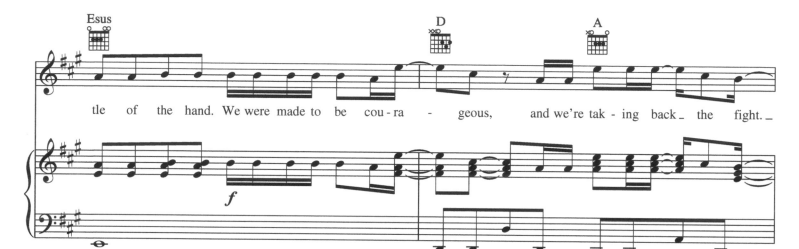

___ We were made to be cou - ra - geous, and it starts with us___ to - night.___

___ The on - ly way___ we'll ev - er stand___ is on our knees___

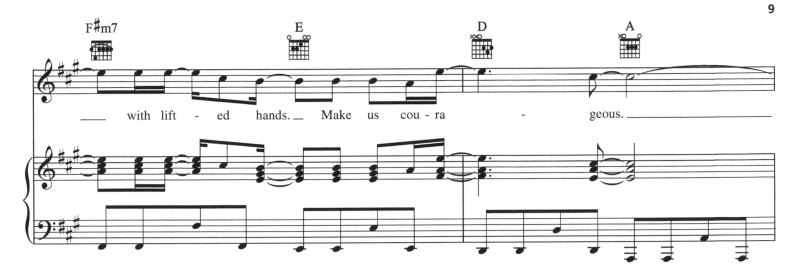

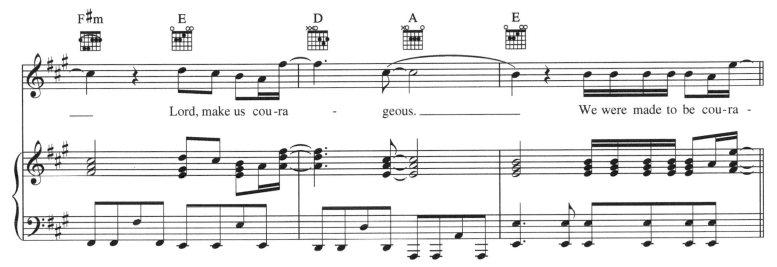

CITY ON THE HILL

Words and Music by MARK HALL
and MATTHEW WEST

Moderate Ballad

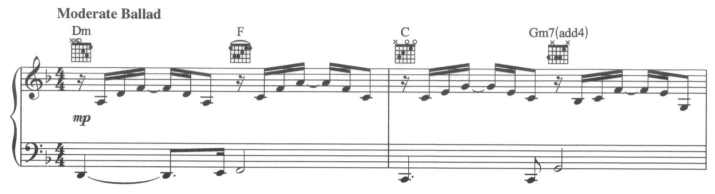

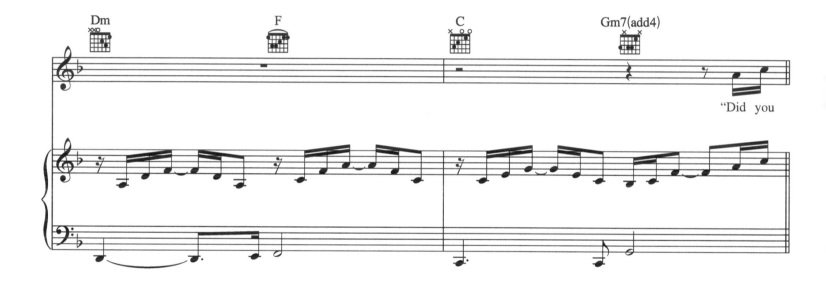

"Did you

hear of the cit-y on the hill?" said one old man__ to the oth-er. It once shined

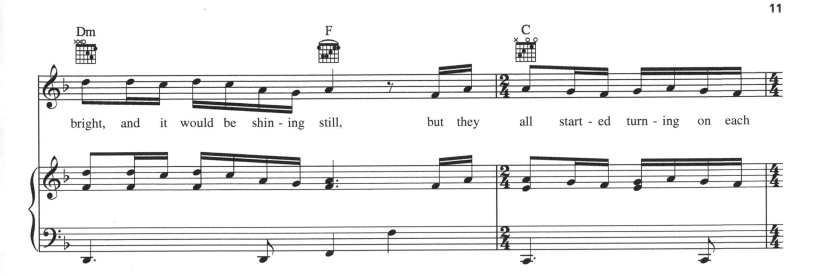

bright, and it would be shin - ing still, but they all start - ed turn - ing on each

oth - er. Mm. _____

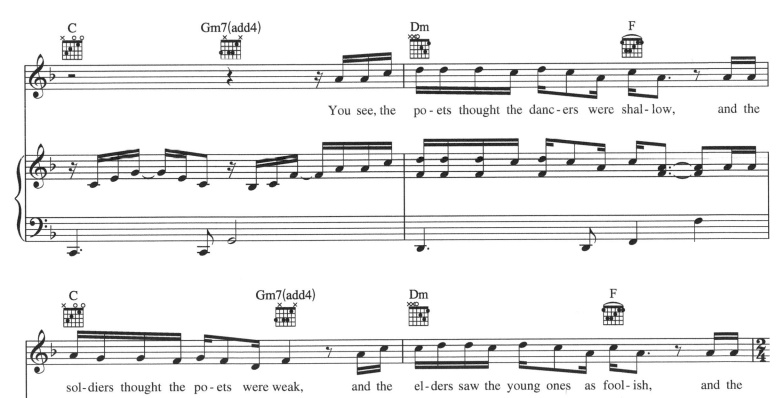

You see, the po - ets thought the danc - ers were shal - low, and the

sol - diers thought the po - ets were weak, and the el - ders saw the young ones as fool - ish, and the

rich man nev - er heard the poor __ man __ speak. And one by __

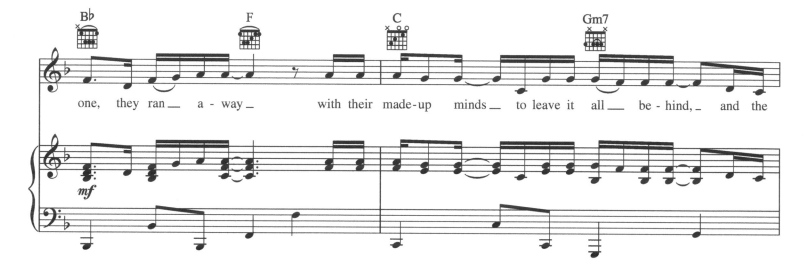

one, they ran __ a - way __ with their made-up minds __ to leave it all __ be - hind, __ and the

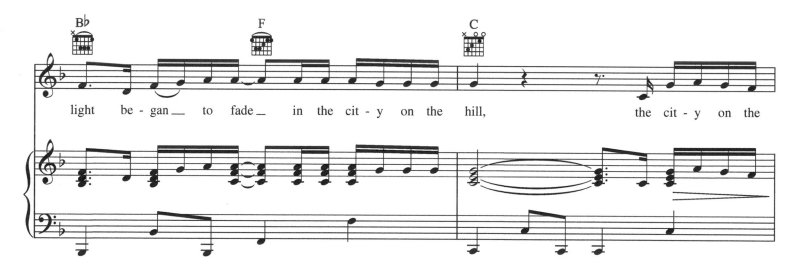

light be - gan __ to fade __ in the cit - y on the hill, the cit - y on the

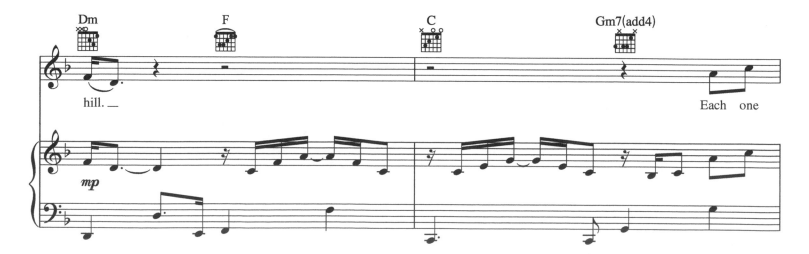

hill. __ Each one

thought that they __ knew bet - ter, but they were dif - f'rent by __ de - sign. __ In-stead of

stand - ing strong _____ to - geth - er, they let their dif - f'renc - es _____ di - vide. __

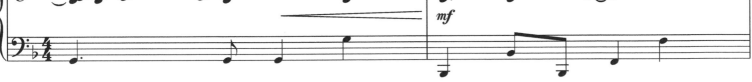

__ And one by __ one, they ran __ a - way __ with their

made - up minds __ to leave it all __ be - hind, __ and the light be - gan __ to fade __ in the cit - y on the

hill,   the cit - y on the hill. __

And the world is search - ing still. __

But it was the   rhy - thm of __ the danc - ers   that
rhy - thm of __ the danc - ers   that

gave the po - ets life.   It was the spir - it of __ the po - ets __ that gave the
gives the po - ets life.   It is the spir - it of __ the po - ets __ that gives the

sol - diers strength _ to fight. ____ It was the fi - re of ___ the young _ ones, it was the
sol - diers strength _ to fight. ____ It is the fi - re of ___ the young _ ones, it is the

wis - dom of ___ the old. _ It was the sto - ry of ___ the poor _ man _ that
wis - dom of ___ the old. _ It is the sto - ry of ___ the poor _ man _ that's

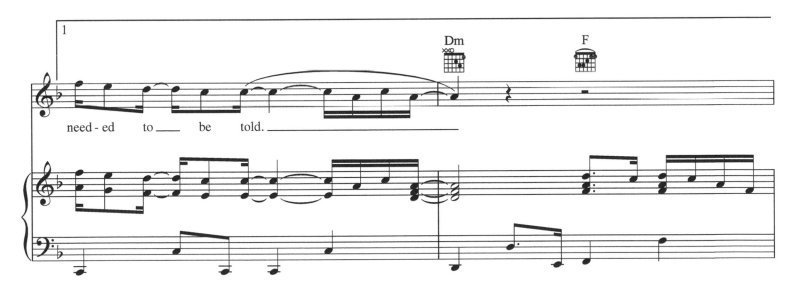

need - ed to _ be told. _____

It is the need-ing to __ be told. __

One by __ one, will we run __ a - way __ with our

made-up minds __ to leave it all __ be-hind, __ as the light be-gins __ to fade __ in the cit - y on the

hill? One by __ one, will we run __ a - way __ with our

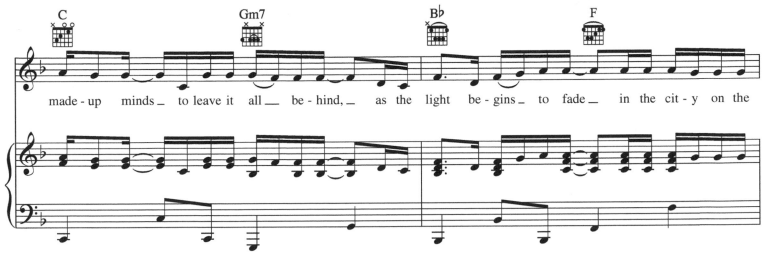

made-up minds __ to leave it all __ be-hind, __ as the light be-gins __ to fade __ in the cit-y on the

hill, the cit - y on the hill? __

And the Fa-ther's call-ing still: ___ Come home _

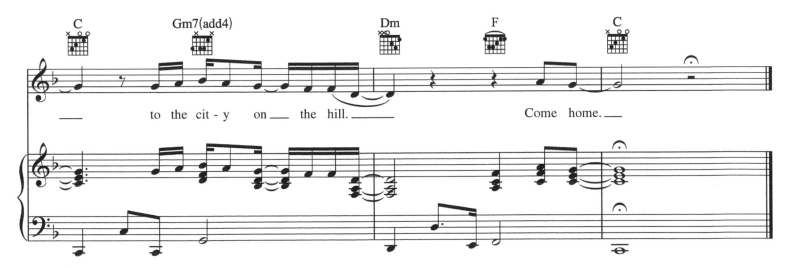

__ to the cit-y on __ the hill. _____ Come home. __

JESUS, FRIEND OF SINNERS

Words and Music by MARK HALL
and MATTHEW WEST

Je-sus, Friend of sin-ners, we have strayed so far a-way.

We cut down peo-ple in Your name, but the sword was

19

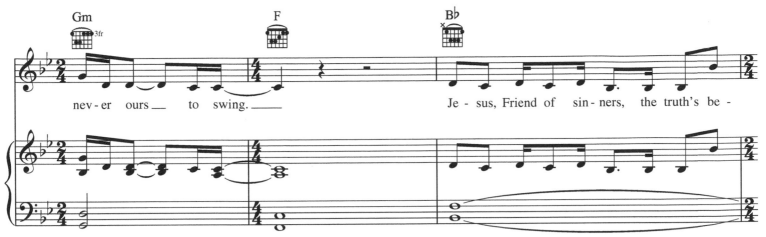

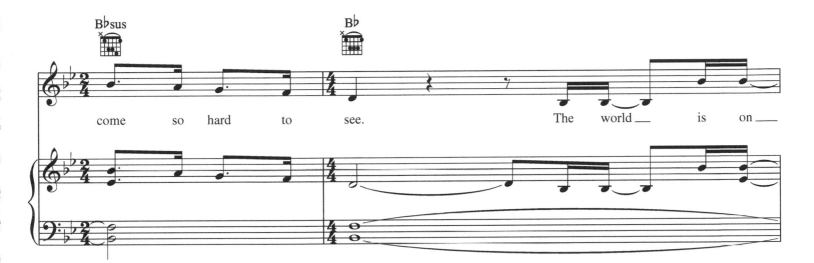

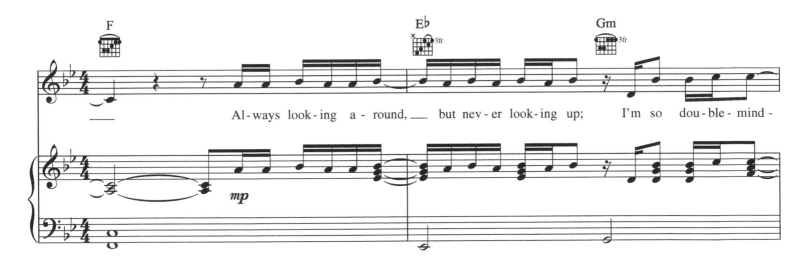

-ed. A plank-eyed saint with dirt-y hands ___ and a heart di-vid-

-ed. Oh, _____ Je - sus, Friend of

sin - ners, ___ o - pen our eyes ___ to the world at the end of our point-ing fin-

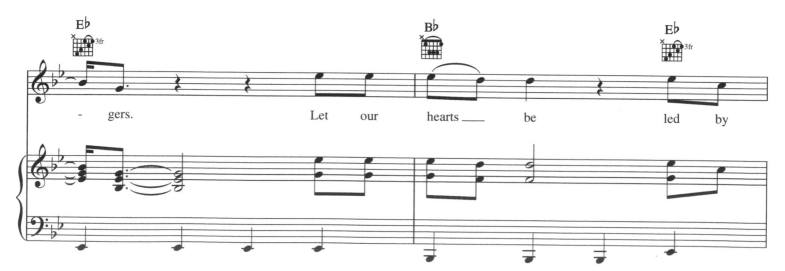

- gers. Let our hearts ___ be led by

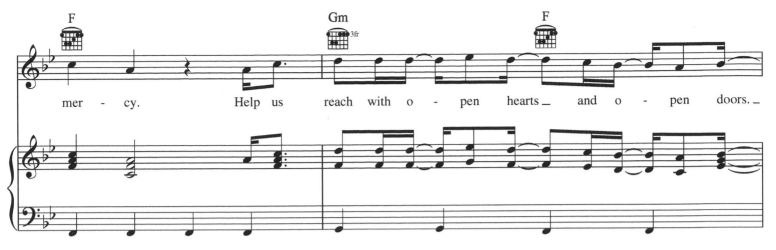

mer - cy. Help us reach with o - pen hearts ___ and o - pen doors. ___

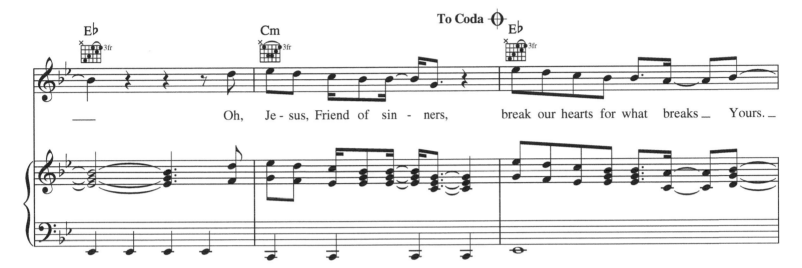

Oh, Je - sus, Friend of sin - ners, break our hearts for what breaks ___ Yours. ___

Yeah, yeah, ___ yeah. ___

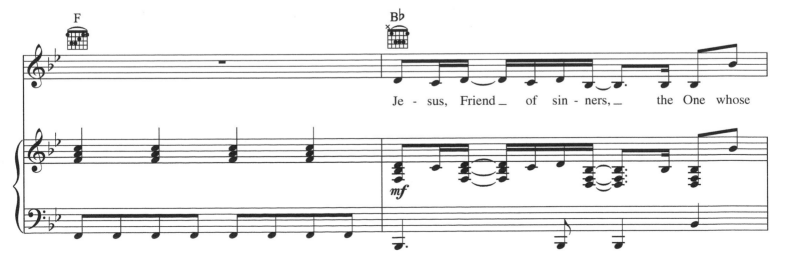

Je - sus, Friend ___ of sin - ners, ___ the One whose

writ - ing in___ the sand___ made the right - eous___ turn a - way___ and the stones___

___ fall from their hands.___ Help us to___ re - mem - ber___ we are

all the least of these.___ Let the mem - 'ry of___ Your mer - cy bring Your

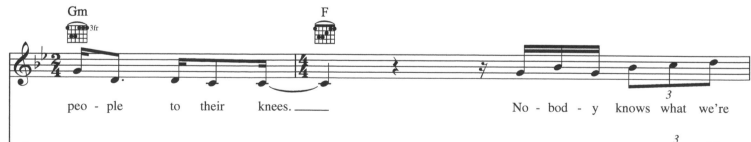

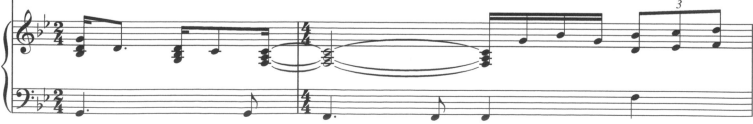

peo - ple to their knees._____ No - bod - y knows what we're

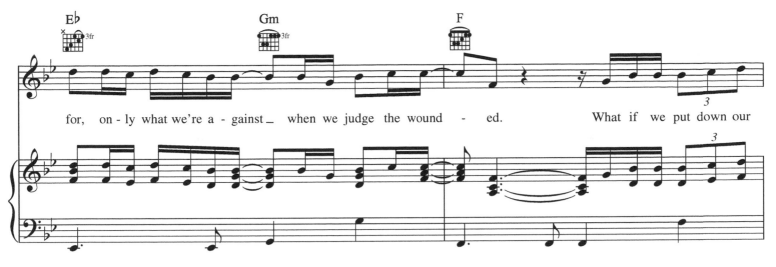

for, on-ly what we're a-gainst ___ when we judge the wound- ed. What if we put down our

signs, crossed o- ver the lines ___ and loved ___ like You ___ did? Oh, ___

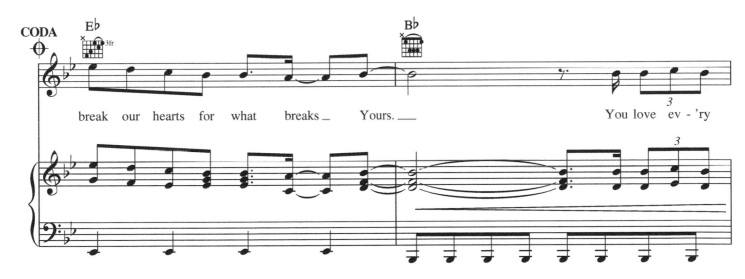

break our hearts for what breaks ___ Yours. ___ You love ev-'ry

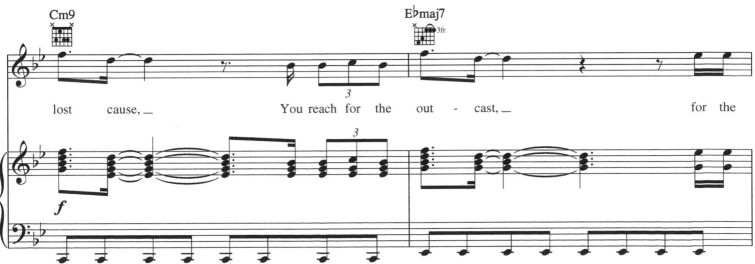

lost cause, ___ You reach for the out- cast, ___ for the

lep - er and — the lame; — they're the rea-son that — You came. — Lord, I was that

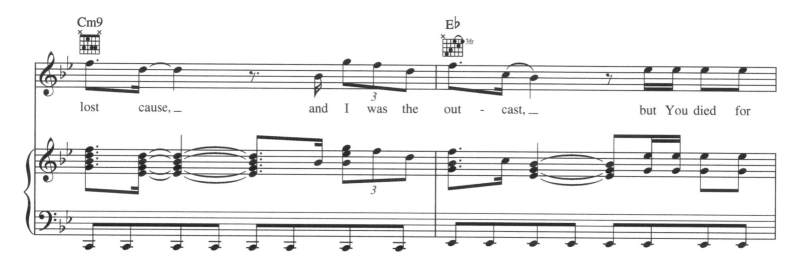

lost cause, — and I was the out - cast, — but You died for

sin - ners just — like me, — a grate - ful lep - er at — Your feet. —

— 'Cause You are — good, You are — good, and Your

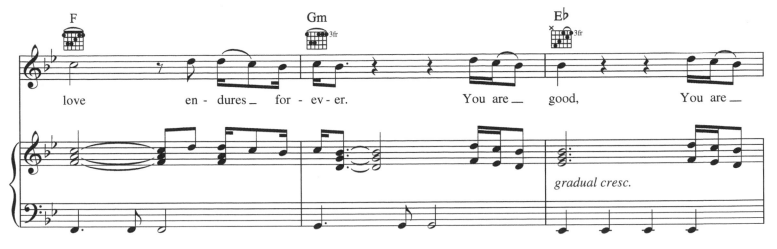

love en-dures for-ev-er. You are __ good, You are __

good, and Your love en-dures for-ev-er. You are __

good, You are good, and Your love en-dures __ for-

ev-er. You are __ good, You are good, and Your

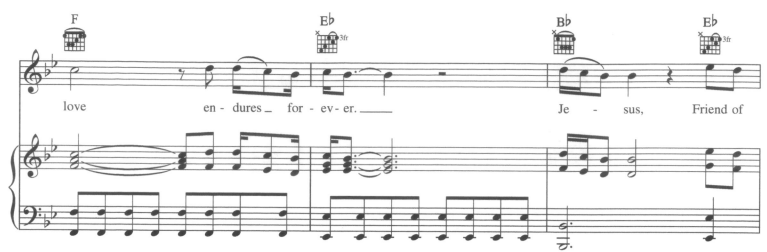

love en - dures _ for - ev - er. _ Je - sus, Friend of

sin - ners, _ o - pen our eyes _ to the world at the end of our point - ing fin -

- gers. _ Let our hearts _ be led by mer - cy. Help us

reach with o - pen hearts _ and o - pen doors. _ Oh, Je - sus, Friend _ of sin - ners,

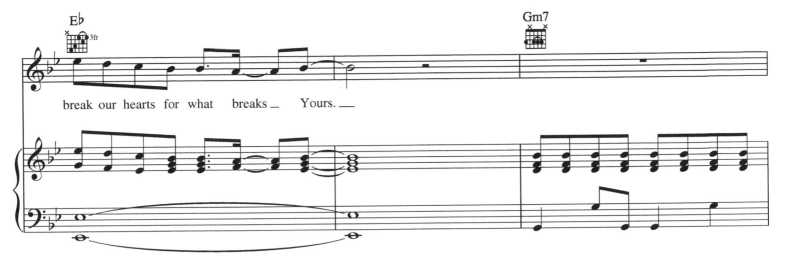

break our hearts for what breaks__ Yours.__

And I was the lost cause,__ and I was the

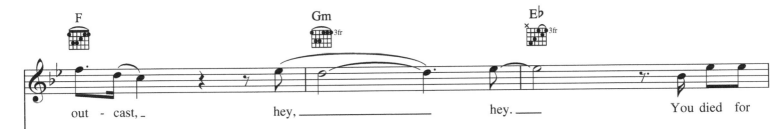

out - cast,__ hey,_____ hey.__ You died for

sin - ners just__ like me,__ a grate - ful lep - er at__ Your feet.__

ALREADY THERE

Words and Music by MARK HALL,
MATTHEW WEST and BERNIE HERMS

Moderately fast

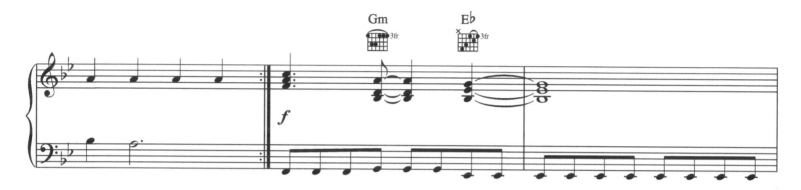

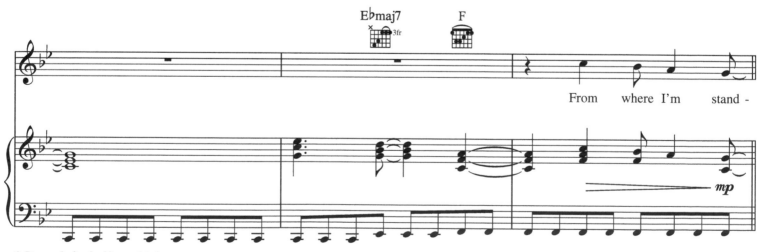

From where I'm stand-

Recorded a half step higher.

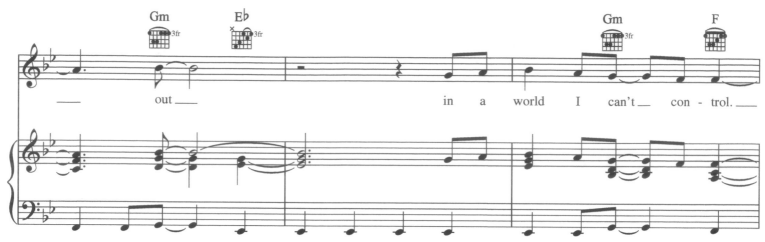

out ___ in a world I can't ___ con - trol. ___

___ Whoa, ___

whoa. ___ When I'm lost in the mys - ter - y,

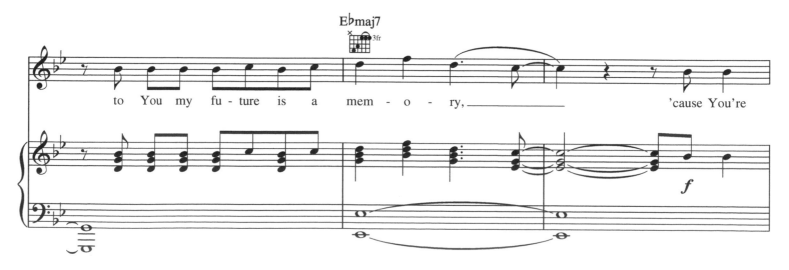

to You my fu - ture is a mem - o - ry, ___ 'cause You're

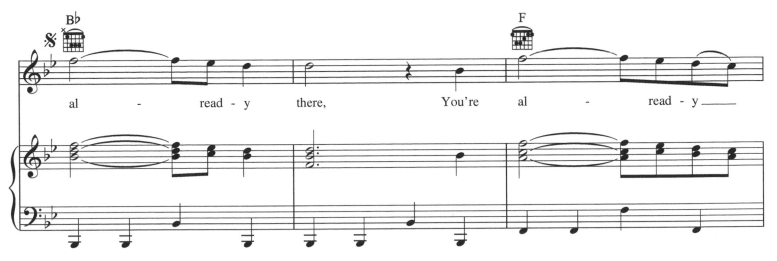

al - read-y there, You're al - read-y ___

there, stand-ing at the end of my life, wait-ing on the

oth - er side. ___ And You're al - read - y

there, You're al - read - y ___ there. ___

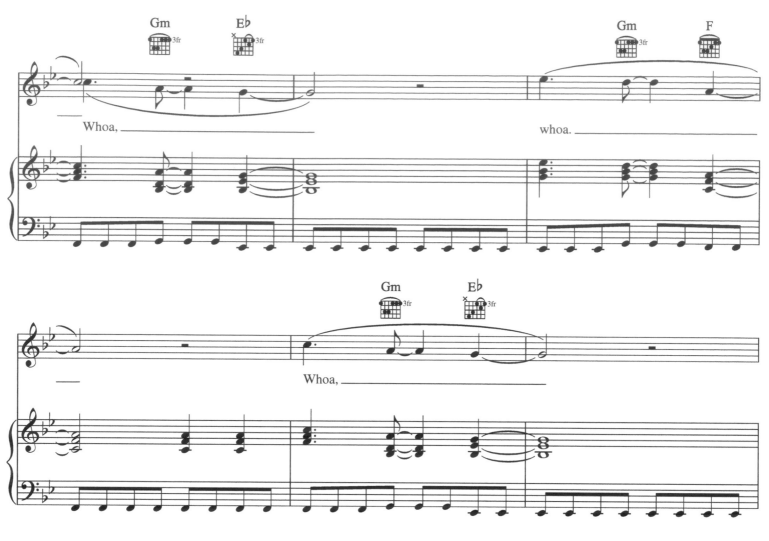

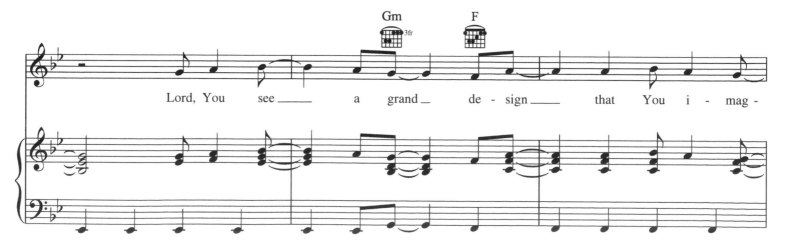

-ined _____ when _ You breathed me in - to life. __

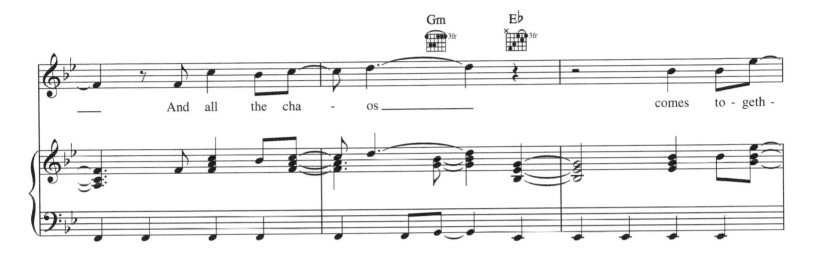

__ And all the cha - os _____ comes to - geth -

- er in __ Your hands __ like a mas - ter - piece, __ hey, _____

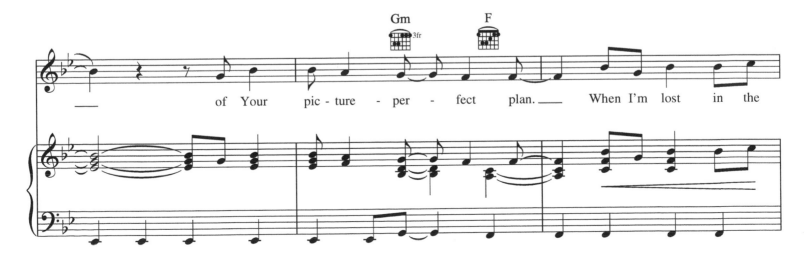

__ of Your pic - ture - per - fect plan. __ When I'm lost in the

Gm

mys - ter - y, to You my fu - ture is a mem - o - ry, _____

E♭

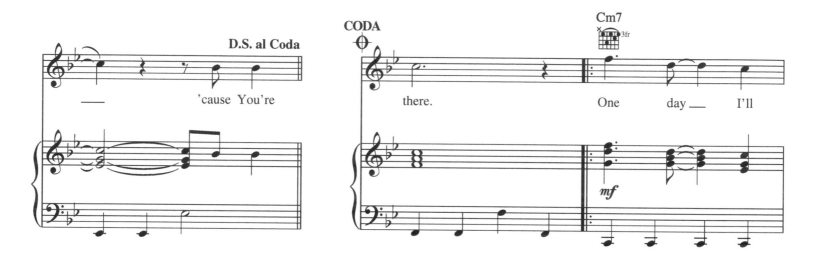

D.S. al Coda

_____ 'cause You're

CODA

there.

Cm7

One day ___ I'll

stand be - fore ___ You and look back ___ on the life I've lived. ___ I

Gm

Cm7

can't wait ___ to en - joy the view ___ and see how ___ all the piec -

1
Gm

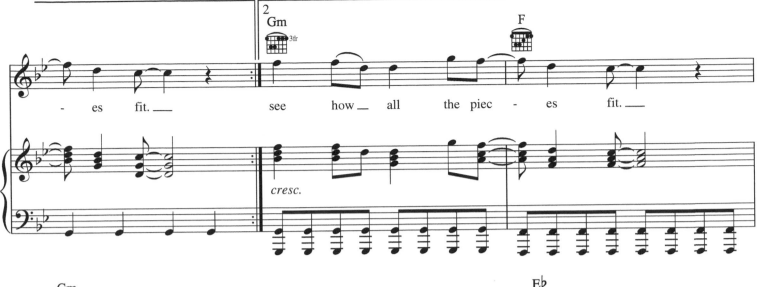

-es fit. __ see how __ all the piec - es fit. __

One day __ I'll stand be - fore __ You and look back __ on the

life I've lived. __ 'Cause You're al - read - y there, You're

al - read - y ___ there. When I'm lost in the mys - ter - y,

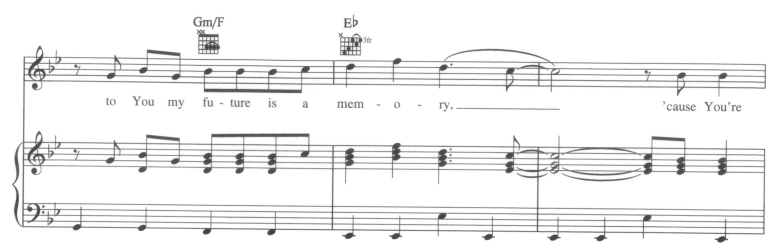

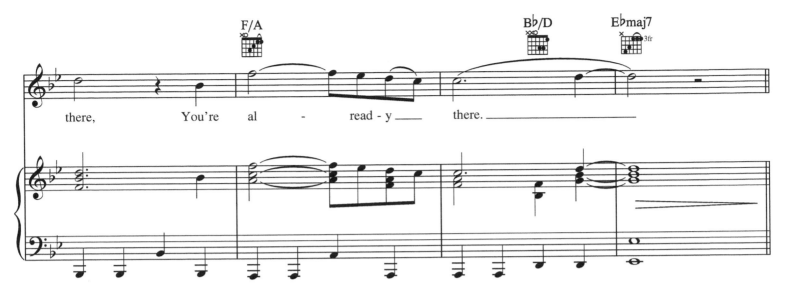

F/A   B♭/D   E♭maj7

there,   You're   al -   read - y _____ there. _____

F   Gm   E♭   Gm   F

mp

Gm   E♭

You're   al -   read - y   there. _____
(Vocal 1st time only)

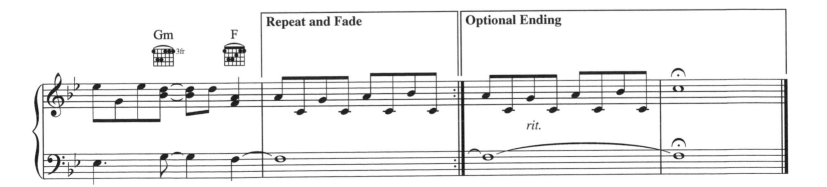

Gm   F

Repeat and Fade   **Optional Ending**

rit.

THE WELL

Words and Music by MARK HALL
and MATTHEW WEST

Moderate Rock Ballad

Leave it all __ be-hind, leave it all __ be-hind, leave it all __ be-

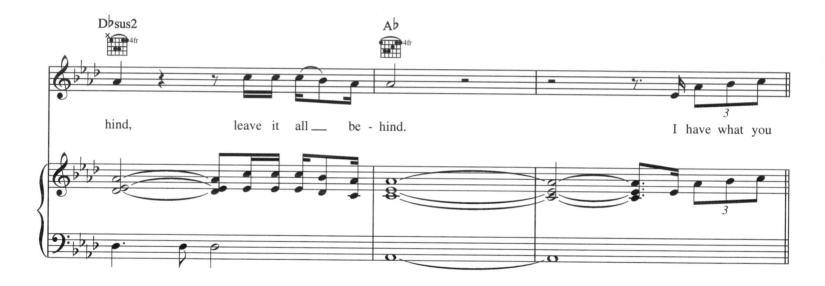

hind, leave it all __ be-hind. I have what you

need, but you keep on ___ search-ing. I've done all the work, but you keep on __

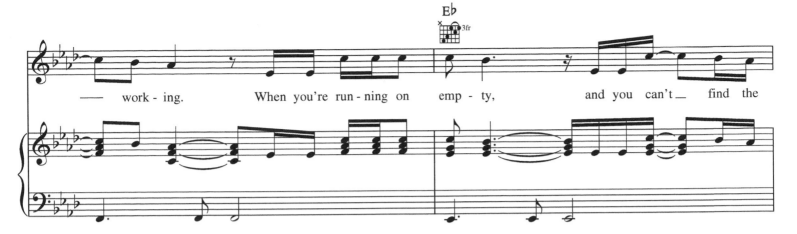

work - ing. When you're run - ning on emp - ty, and you can't__ find the

rem - e - dy,____ just come__ to the well.

You can spend your whole__ life chas - ing what's__

___ miss - ing, but that emp - ty in - side,_____ it just ain't gon - na__

So leave it all ____ be-hind ____ and come ____ to the

well. ____ So bring Me your heart, ____ no mat-ter how ____

____ bro - ken. Just come as you are _____ when your last prayer is ____

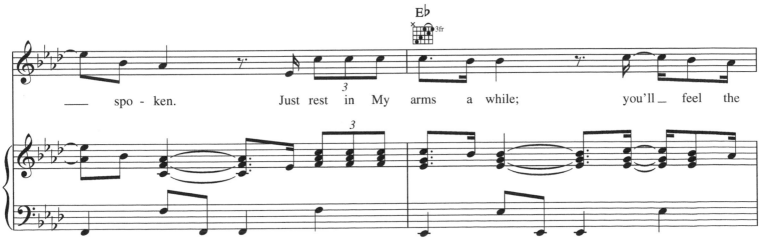

____ spo - ken. Just rest in My arms a while; you'll ___ feel the

D.S. al Coda

change, My child, _____ when you come _ to the well. And all who

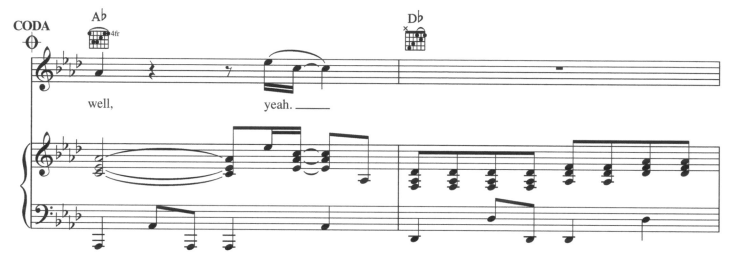

CODA

well, yeah. _____

Leave it all _____ be - hind. _____

The world will try, but it can _ nev - er

fill. _____ Leave it all _____ be-hind, And now that you're

full of love be-yond _____ meas-ure, _____ your joy's gon-na

flow like a stream in the des-ert. _____ Soon all the

world _ will see that liv-ing wa-ter is found in Me, _ 'cause you've come _____ to the

well, yeah. _____ And all who

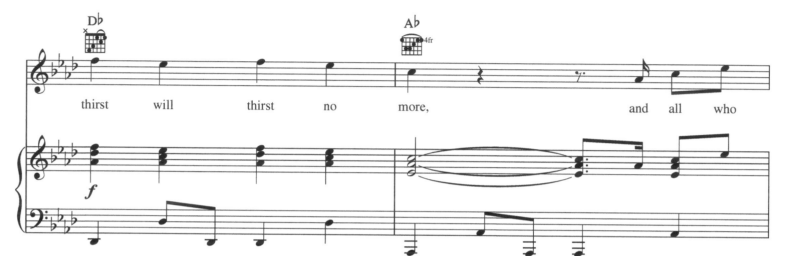

thirst will thirst no more, and all who

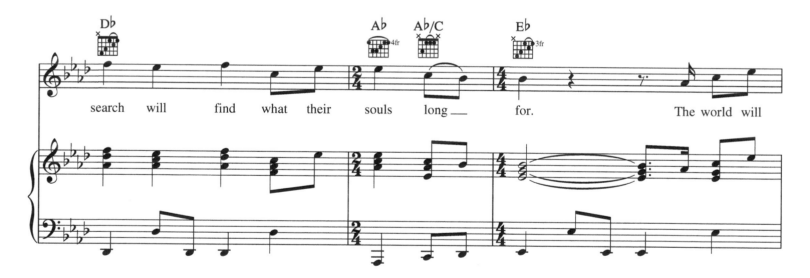

search will find what their souls long ___ for. The world will

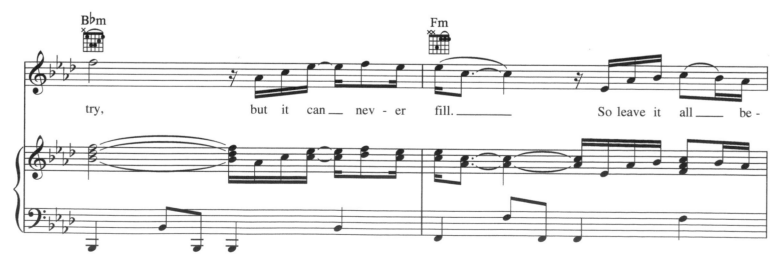

try, but it can ___ nev - er fill. _____ So leave it all ___ be -

hind and come _____ to the well. Leave it all _____ be -

hind and come _____ to the well. Leave it all _____ be -

hind, leave it all _____ be - hind, leave it all _____ be -
(2nd time see additional lyrics)

hind, leave it all _____ be - hind. _____ Leave it all _____ be -

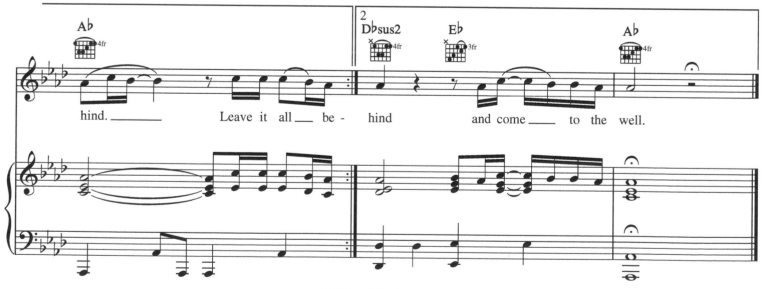

Additional Lyrics
(Background)

Your pursuit of perfection, (leave it all behind.)
Your fear of rejection, (leave it all behind.)
Your temporary pleasures, (leave it all behind.)
All your earthly treasures, (leave it all behind.)
Dried-up, empty religion, (leave it all behind.)
Rusty chains of addiction, (leave it all behind.)
All the guilt that weighs you down, (leave it all behind.)
Just leave it all behind and come to the well.

SPIRIT WIND

Words and Music by MARK HALL
and JASON HOARD

Easy Country feel

E - ze - ki - el____ stared down in - to the val - ley ____ filled with dry ___ bones bak - ing in ___ the sun, ___ ___ re - mains that used to be ___ a might - y

* *Recorded a half step lower.*

ar - my. ___ To him, it looked ___ like their fight-ing days were

done. ___ But driv-en by a call - ing on ___ his

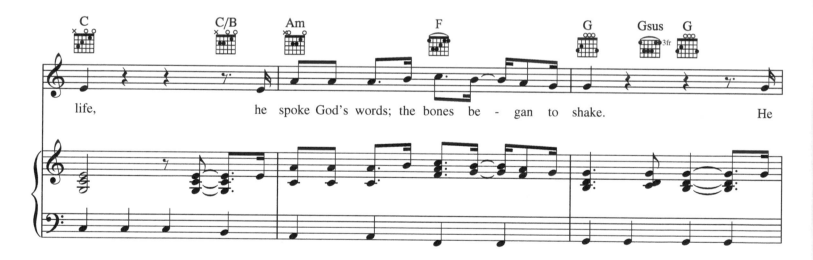

life, he spoke God's words; the bones be - gan to shake. He

stared wide - eyed as the flesh be - gan ___ to form. ___ And as he proph-e - sied ___ to the wind, ___

the sol - diers be - gan to wake. _____ And the

Lord sent __ His wind in - to the val - ley, __ and
Lord, send __ Your wind in - to this val - ley, __ and

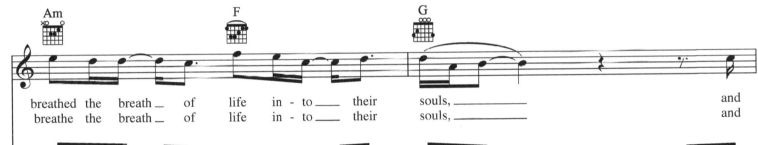

breathed the breath __ of life in - to __ their souls, _____ and
breathe the breath __ of life in - to __ their souls, _____ and

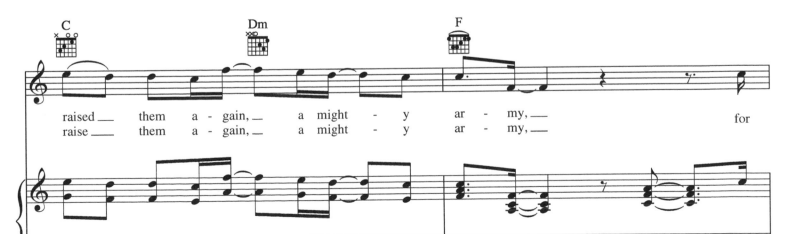

raised __ them a - gain, __ a might - y ar - my, __ for
raise __ them a - gain, __ a might - y ar - my, __

soon these a - ris - en war - riors will bat - tle a - gain, _____ for

they have __ been filled __ with the Spir - it _____ Wind. Whoa, _____

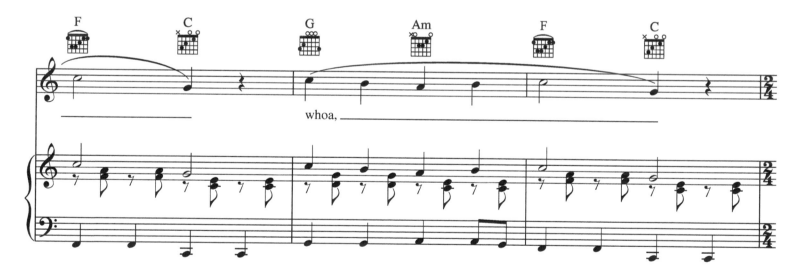

whoa, _____

whoa. _____

A

pas - tor stands be - fore __ his con - gre - ga - tion, __

once a might - y ar - my for the Lord. _____ But

now he stares __ in - to the life - less eyes, __ be - liev - ers lead - ing car - nal lives. __

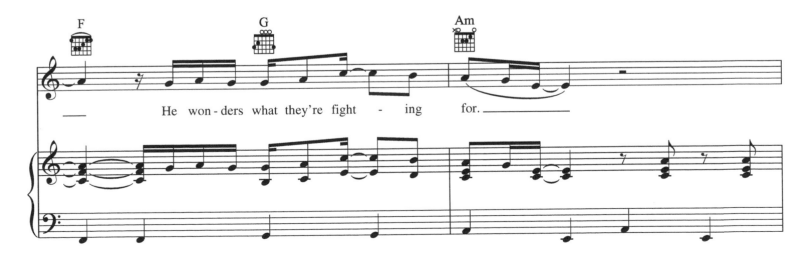

__ He won - ders what they're fight - ing for. _____

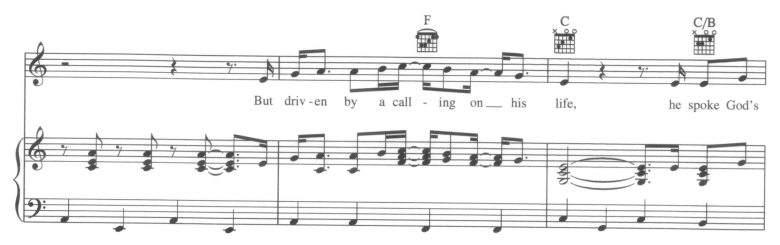

But driv-en by a call-ing on___ his life, he spoke God's

Word like he'd done a hun-dred times be - fore._____ But

this time, he comes bro - ken ___ and weep-ing,___ with tears of a bro-ken heart, _

D.S. al Coda

___ and he cries out___ to the Lord:_____ Oh,

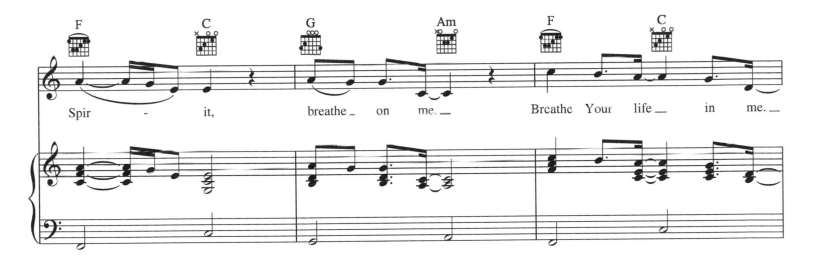

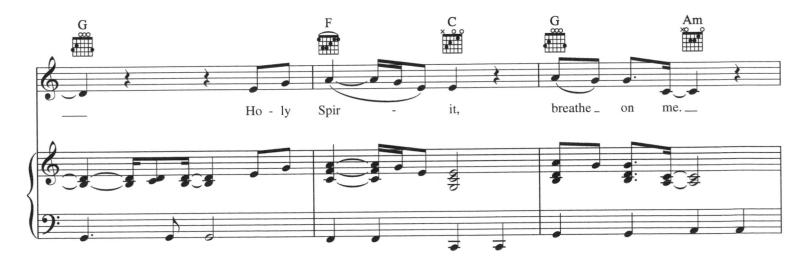

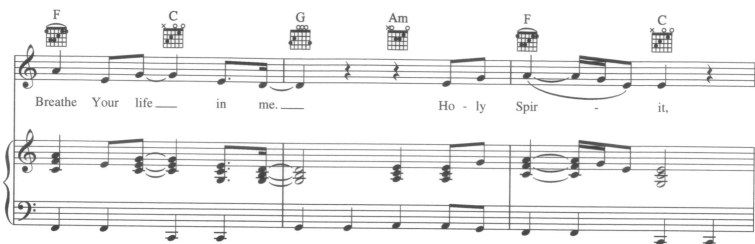

Breathe Your life __ in me. __ Ho - ly Spir - it,

breathe __ on me. __ Breathe Your life __ in me. __ Ho - ly Spir - it, __

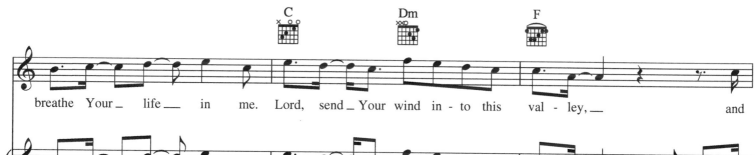

breathe Your __ life __ in me. Lord, send __ Your wind in - to this val - ley, __ and

breathe the breath __ of life in - to __ our souls, __ and raise __ us a - gain, __ a might - y

ar - my, _____ for soon these a - ris - en war - riors will bat - tle a - gain. ___

_____ We have _ been filled _ with the Spir - it ____ Wind. Whoa, __

(Vocal ad lib. on repeats)

whoa, _____

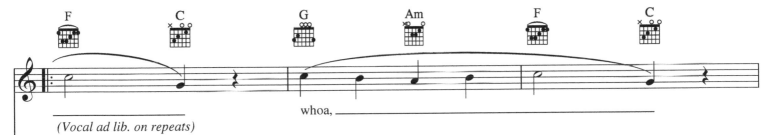

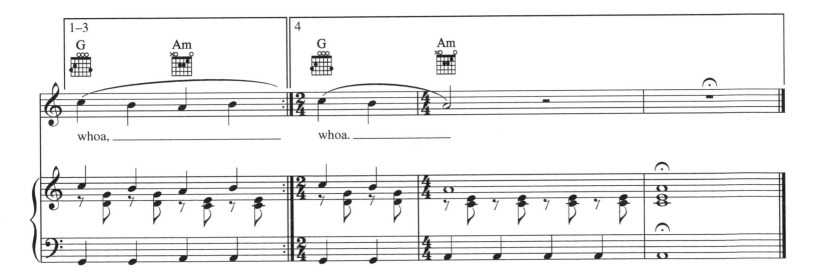

1–3

whoa, _____ whoa. _____

JUST ANOTHER BIRTHDAY

Words and Music by MARK HALL
and TOM DOUGLAS

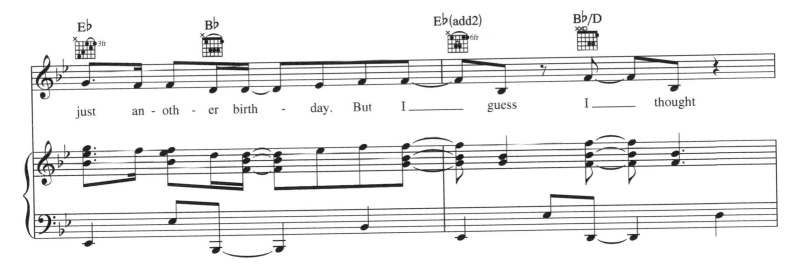

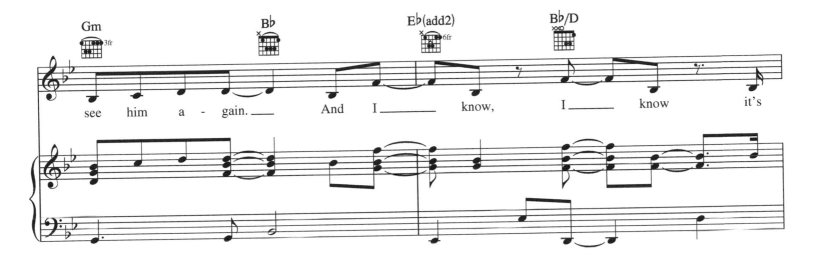

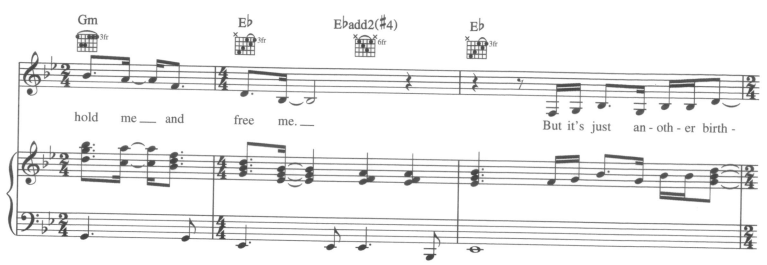

hold me __ and free me. __ But it's just an - oth - er birth -

- day, __ and I'll be __ fine. __

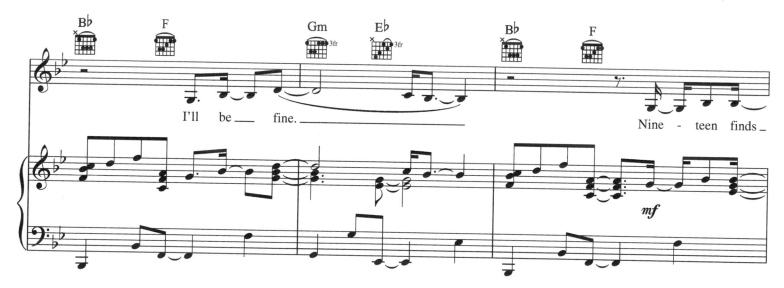

I'll be __ fine. _____ Nine - teen finds __

__ me, and I'm wild - eyed and wide o - pen. I gave my -

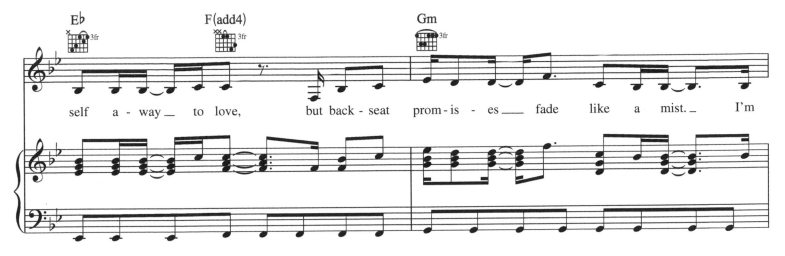

self a-way to love, but back-seat prom-is-es fade like a mist. I'm

scream-ing at the mid-night air. Ev-'ry-one hears me, but I don't care. My heart's

clenched just like a fist, 'cause, peo-ple, I did-n't ask for an-y of this. And I

know, I know it's just an-oth-er birth-day. But I

60

guess I ___ thought this would be the one ___ when he would call ___

me, see ___ me, ___ hold me ___ and free me. ___

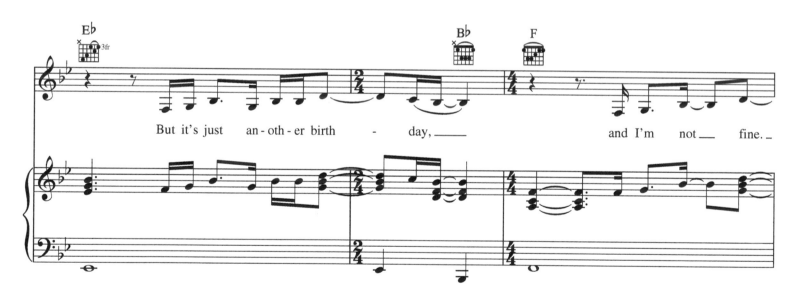

But it's just an-oth-er birth - day, ___ and I'm not ___ fine. ___

I'm not ___ fine. ___

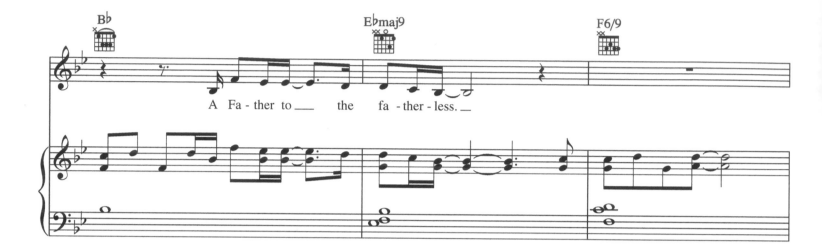

A Fa-ther to ___ the fa-ther-less. ___

Twen-ty-one ___ finds me ___ blow-ing out

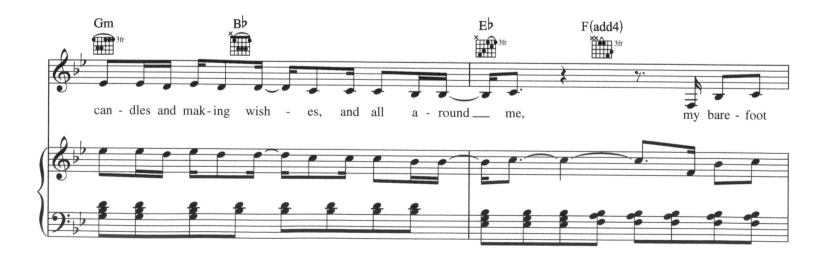

can-dles and mak-ing wish-es, and all a-round ___ me, my bare-foot

prin-cess twirls _ and sings. _ It's so a - maz _ - ing, _ look-ing

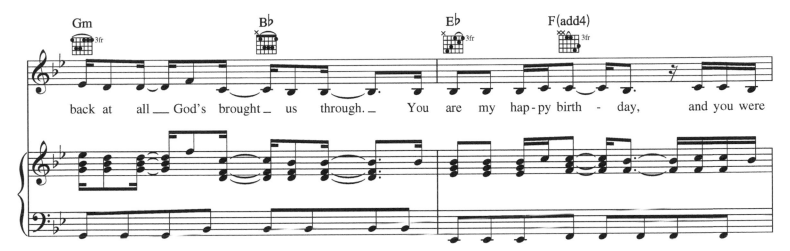

back at all _ God's brought _ us through. _ You are my hap-py birth - day, and you were

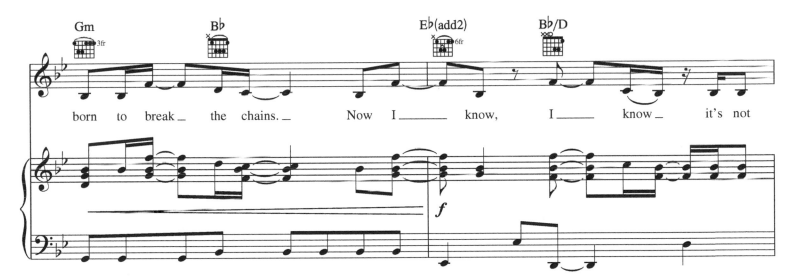

born to break _ the chains. _ Now I _ know, I _ know _ it's not

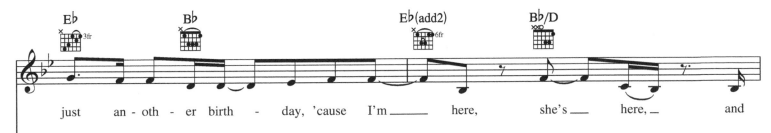

just an - oth - er birth - day, 'cause I'm _ here, she's _ here, _ and

look how far we've come since You've called me, saw me,

held me and freed me. Thank You, Lord, for an-oth-er birth-

-day, and we'll be fine.

mf

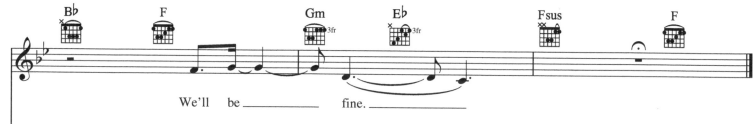

We'll be fine.

rit.

WEDDING DAY

Words and Music by MARK HALL,
NICHOLE NORDEMAN and BERNIE HERMS

Moderately

There's a stir - ring ___ in the throne ___ room, ___ and all cre-

a - tion holds ___ its ___ breath, wait - ing now ___ to see the Bride-

- groom, ___ won-d'ring how ___ the bride ___ will ___ dress. And she ___ wears

Recorded a half step lower.

white.
And she knows
that she's un-de-serv-

-ing;____ she bears the shame____ of his-to-ry.____ But this

worn
and wea-ry maid - en____ is not the bride____ that He____

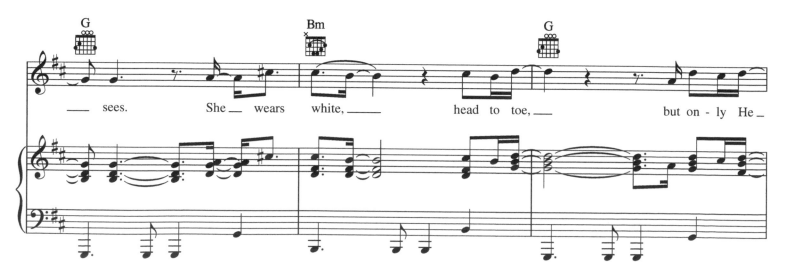

____ sees.
She__ wears white,____ head to toe,___ but on - ly He__

could make __ it so. When some-one dries your tears, __ when

some-one wins __ your heart __ and says you're beau - ti - ful __ when

you don't know __ you are, __ when all you __ long to see __ is

writ-ten on __ His face, love has come __ and fi - n'lly set __ you free __ on that wed-ding day, __

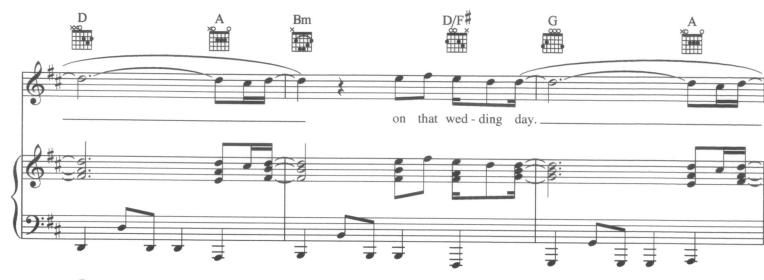

on that wed - ding day.

She __ has danced __ in gold - en cas - tles, _____ she has

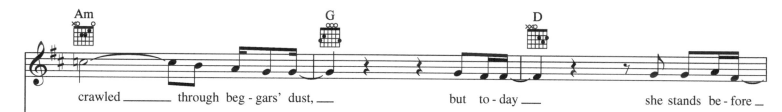

crawled _____ through beg - gars' dust, ___ but to - day ___ she stands be - fore __

__ Him _____ and she wears _____ His right - eous - ness. She __ will

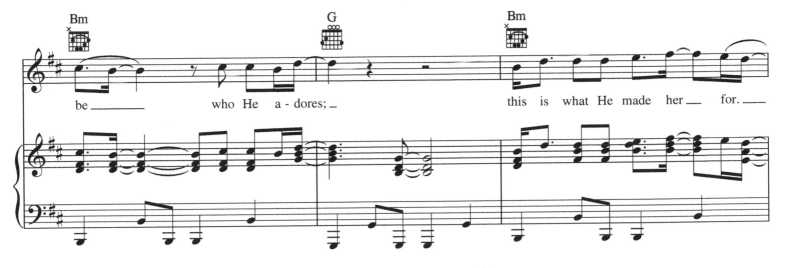

be _____ who He a - dores; __ this is what He made her __ for. __

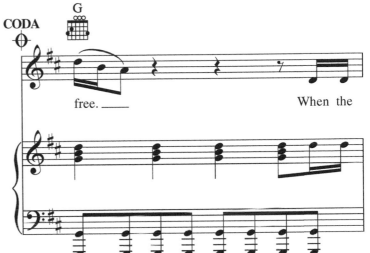

D.S. al Coda

When some-one

CODA

free. __ When the

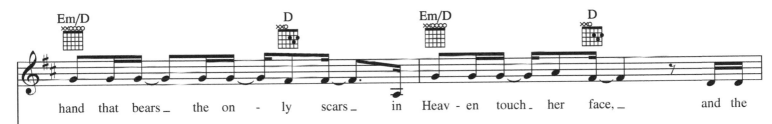

hand that bears __ the on - ly scars __ in Heav - en touch __ her face, __ and the

last tears __ she'll ev - er cry __ are fi - n'lly wiped __ a - way, __ and the

clouds roll back as He takes her hand __ and walks her through the gates, __ for-

ev - er we __ will reign. _____ When some-one dries your tears, __ when

some-one wins __ your heart __ and says you're beau - ti - ful __ when

you don't know __ you are, __ when all you __ long to see __ is

ANGEL

Words and Music by MARK HALL,
MATTHEW WEST and BERNIE HERMS

It was a day just like an-y oth-er day.

I was a boy ___ just like ev-'ry oth-er boy, ___ when a girl un-like an-

G/B — Am

-y I ___ had seen, ___ it's like she stepped out ___ of a dream ___ and

Fmaj7 — Fsus2

in - to my ___ world. ___ It could-'ve been the sum - mer wind ___

G — F

___ play - ing with her ___ hair. ___ As the sun danced in her eyes, ___

G — F

___ we were stand - ing ___ there. ___ She smiled; ___ I for-got ___ my name, ___

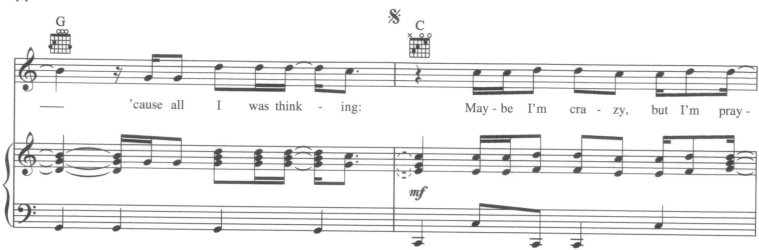

'cause all I was think - ing: May - be I'm cra - zy, but I'm pray -

- ing that an an - gel __ will love __ me, __ an an - gel __ will love __ me.

May - be I'm a fool, but I'm __ still fall - ing, ask - ing Heav - en __ a - bove __

To Coda

__ me for an an - gel __ to love __ me __ the rest of my __ life, __

just be-gun __ to fall, __ and from the deep-est part __ of me, __ I say, __ "I do."

D.S. al Coda

CODA

__ me. And af-ter all __ the chang-ing sea-

- sons have turned to __ years, __ the crowds are gone __ and the songs __ have fad-

- ed, well, I'll still be __ here, hold-ing you __ and thank-ing Heav-

-en for my an-gel. May-be I'm cra-zy, but I'm pray-

-ing that an an-gel __ will love __ me, __ an an-gel __ will love __

__ me. Well, may-be I'm cra- zy _____ for pray-ing an

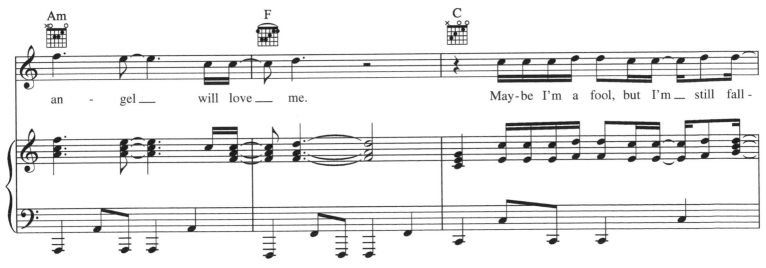

an-gel __ will love __ me. May-be I'm a fool, but I'm __ still fall-

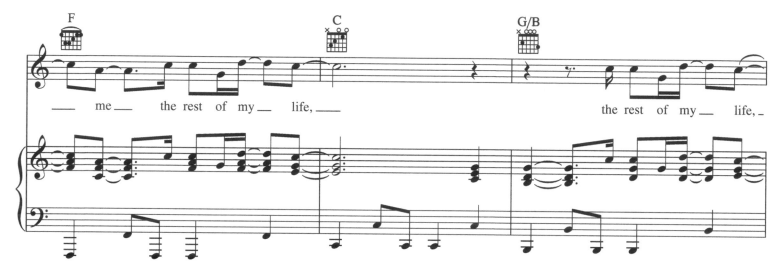

MY OWN WORST ENEMY

Words and Music by MARK HALL
and MATTHEW WEST

Driving Rock beat

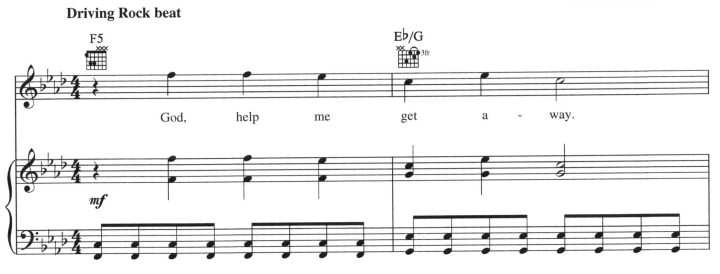

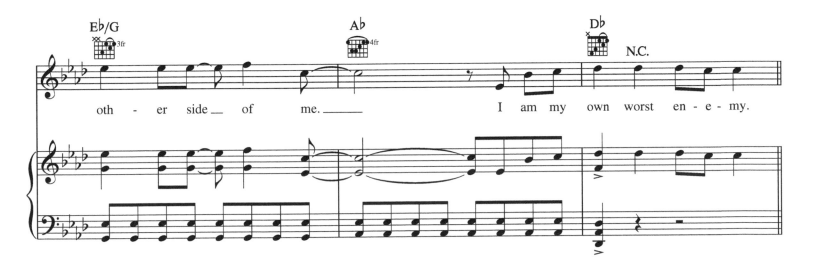

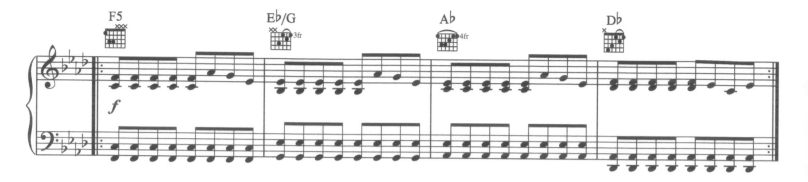

I caught a glimpse in my rear-view mir-ror
I'll take a step and it's right___ be-hind___ me,

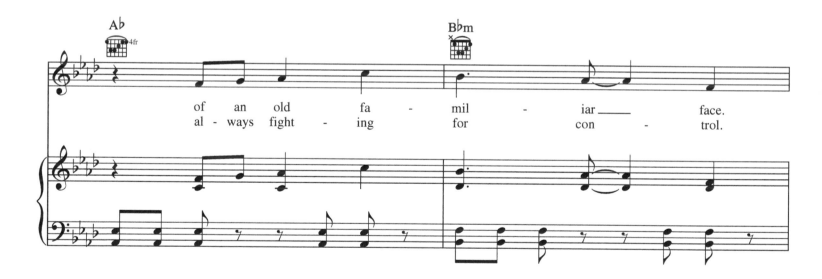

of an old fa-mil-iar___ face.
al-ways fight-ing for con-trol.

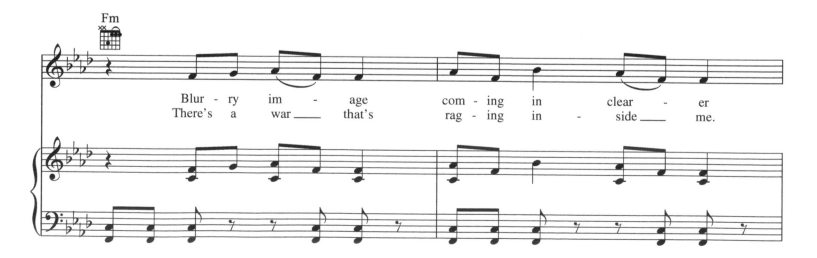

Blur-ry im-age com-ing in clear-er
There's a war___ that's rag-ing in-side___ me.

of a past   I   can't   for   e -   rase.
I feel the bat - tle   for   my   soul.

I could-'ve sworn   I   put him in the ground,
It's like my shad - ow is   drag-ging me a - round,

but looks like he's   found his way   out.   God, help me
and You are my   on - ly way   out,

get a - way.   Break the chains and   set me   free

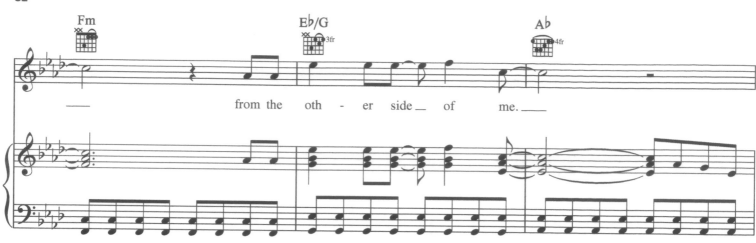

from the oth - er side __ of __ me. __

I can't fight this fight a - lone.

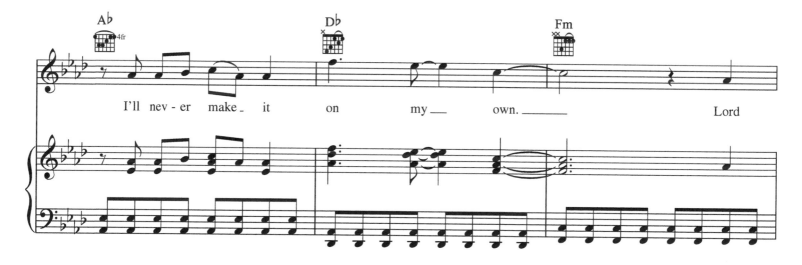

I'll nev - er make __ it on my __ own. _____ Lord

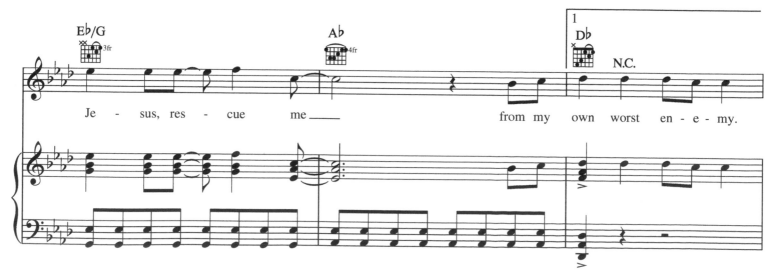

Je - sus, res - cue me _____ from my own worst en - e - my.

own worst en - e - my. ____

____ Lord, help __ me ____ feed the life __

____ I'm try - ing to live, ____ and starve the life ____ I'm trying to leave. __

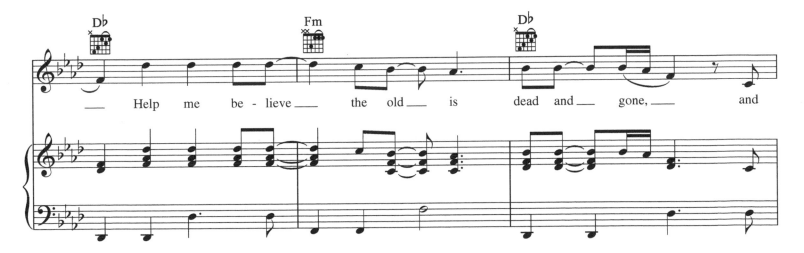

____ Help me be - lieve ____ the old __ is ____ dead and __ gone, ____ and

I am a new cre - a - tion. God, help __ me

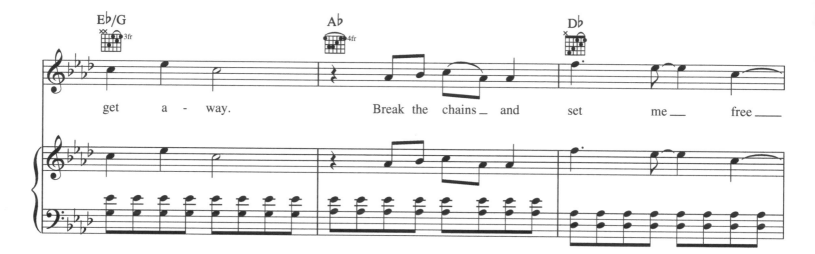

get a - way. Break the chains __ and set me __ free __

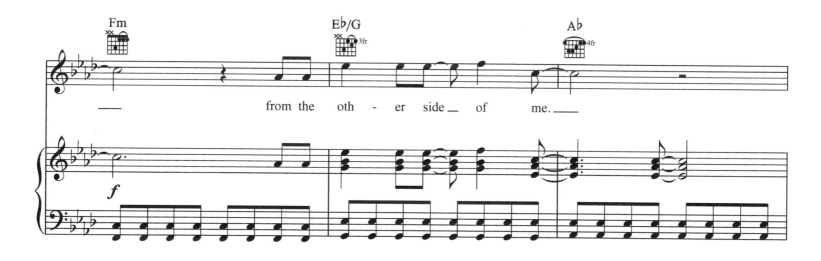

__ from the oth - er side __ of me. __

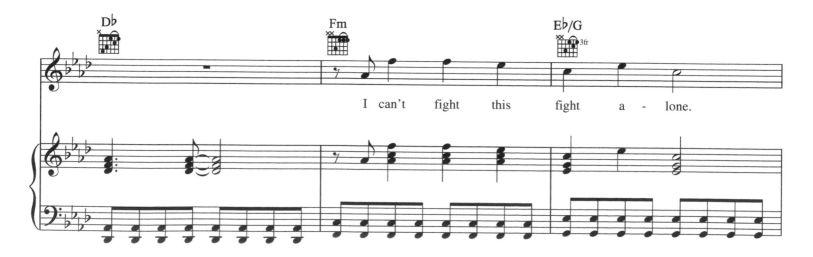

I can't fight this fight a - lone.

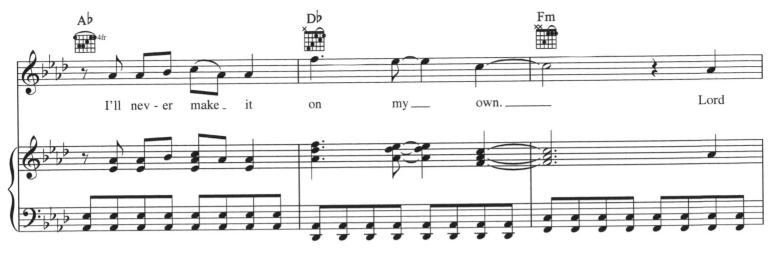

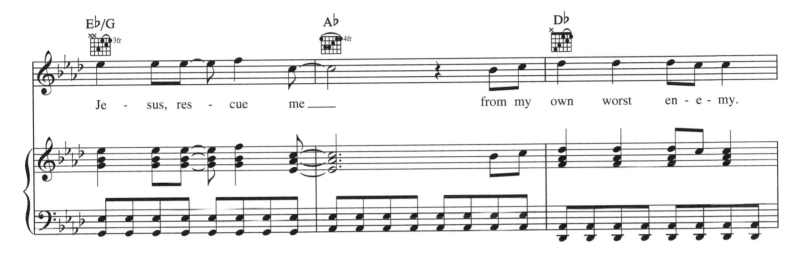

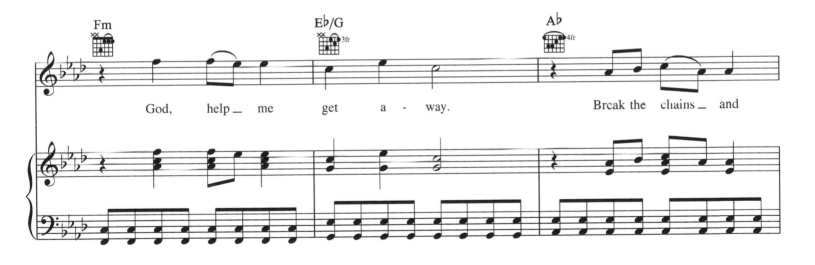

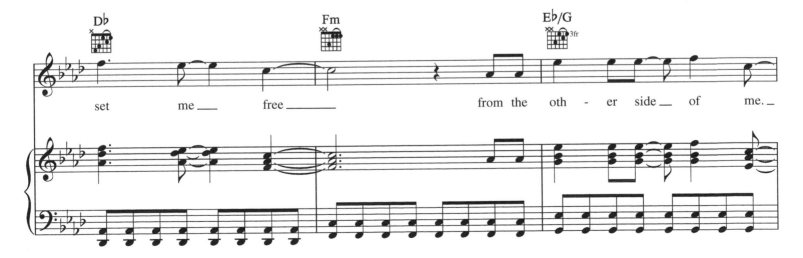

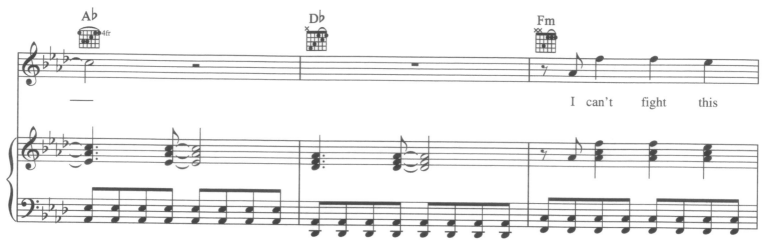

I can't fight this

fight a - lone. I'll nev - er make it on my own.

Lord Je - sus, res - cue me

from my own worst en - e - my.

FACE DOWN

Words and Music by HECTOR CERVANTES
and MARC BYRD

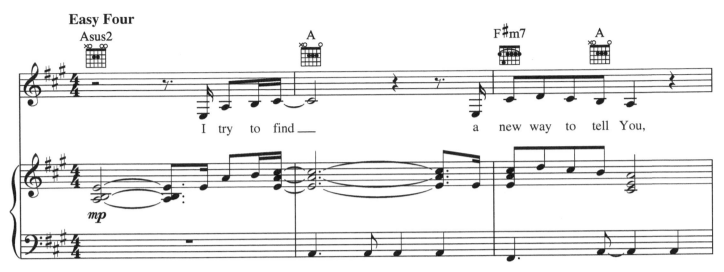

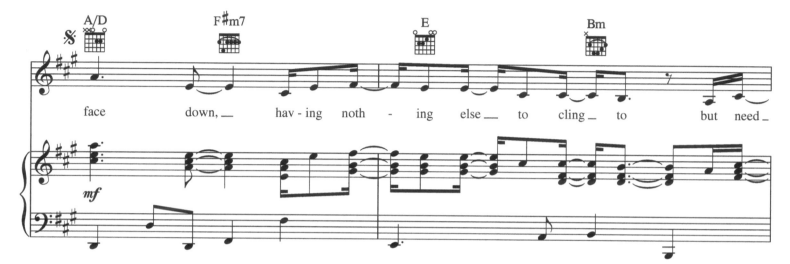

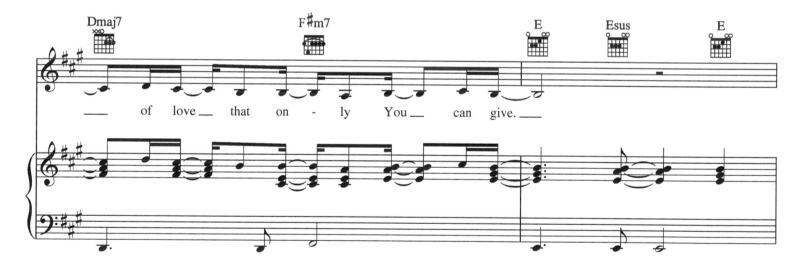

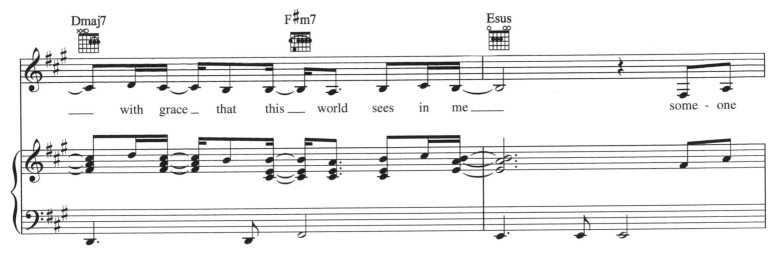

with grace that this world sees in me _____ some - one

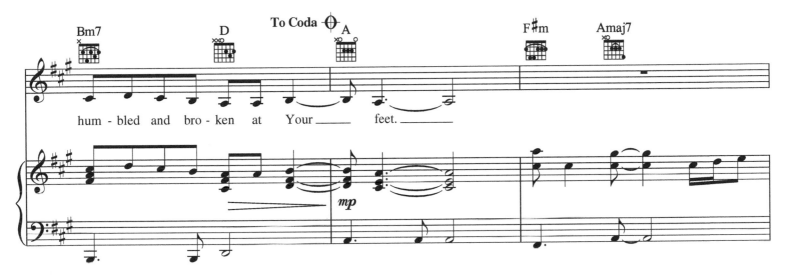

hum - bled and bro - ken at Your _____ feet. _____

mp

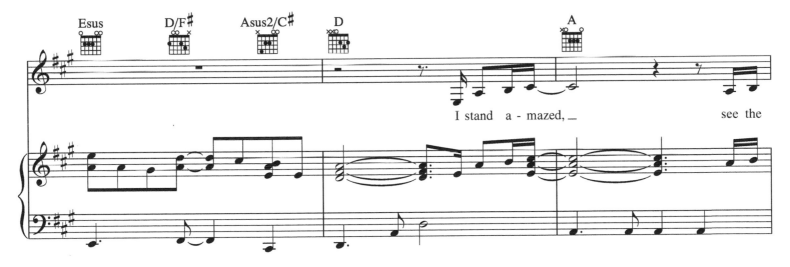

I stand a - mazed, _____ see the

work of Your hands. _____ Still, I _____ don't un - der - stand _____ why You would res -

-cue me.___ An emp-ty cross where You

suf-fered and bled,____ o-ver-com-ing my death,____ re-cre-at-

D.S. al Coda

-ing me.___ With this free - dom, I___ will be_____

CODA

___ feet._____ So I'm ask - ing for__ Your help;__ I just can't do__

this by my-self. After all, this life's for You and not for me.

Through Your mer-cy, now I see bro-ken-ness

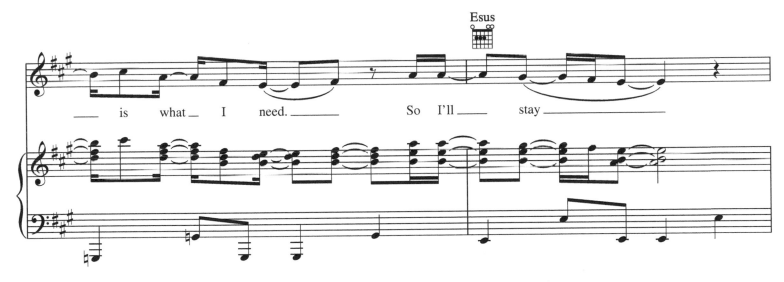

is what I need. So I'll stay

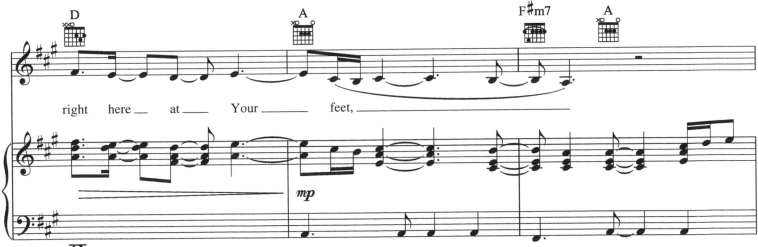

right here at Your feet,

right here at _____ Your feet, _____ and

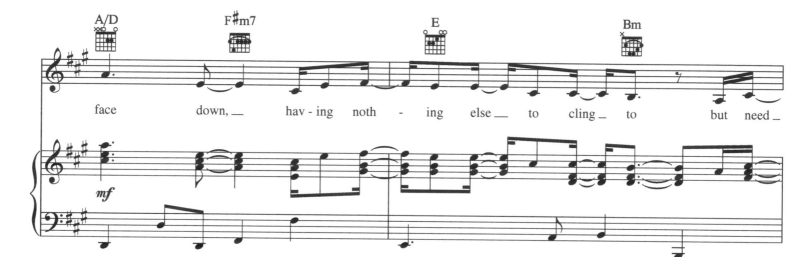

face down, __ hav-ing noth - ing else __ to cling __ to but need __

__ of love __ that on - ly You __ can give. __

Face down, __ where I know __ that I __ be - long, __ and I pray __

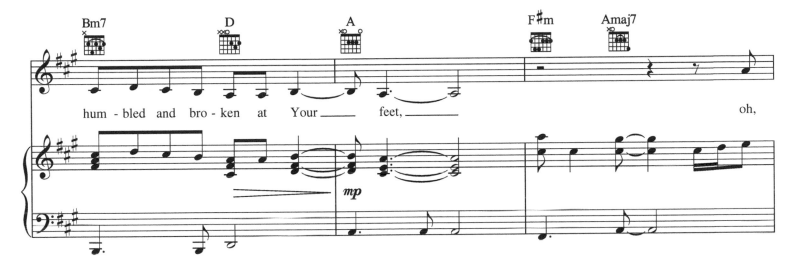

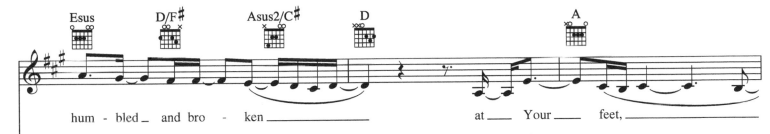

SO FAR TO FIND YOU

Words and Music by MARK HALL
and STEVEN CURTIS CHAPMAN

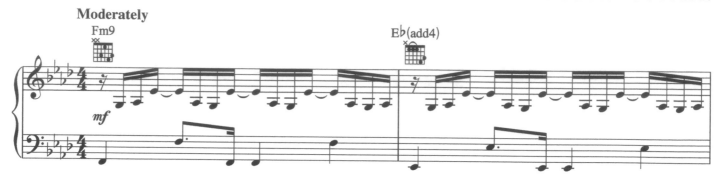

You were bro - ken, _____ a-

ban - doned, _____ and cry - ing _____ all a - lone. _____

We were wait - ing ___ and

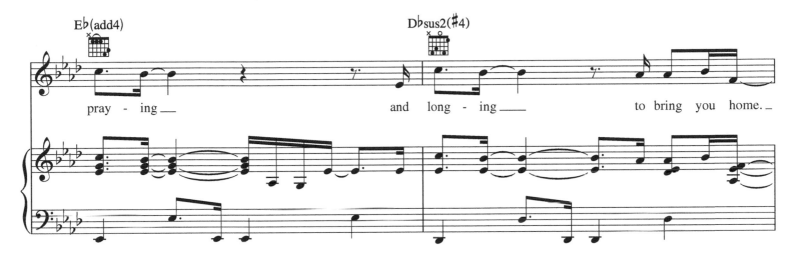

pray - ing ___ and long - ing ___ to bring you home. ___

And then ___ we saw your face. ___

In a mo - ment, you ___ were wrapped ___ up in ___ our hearts. ___

We took __ a step of faith, ___ and now

here we are. ___ Will you let me hold __ you in __ my

arms to - night? __ I have come __ so far to find __ you, so

far to find __ you. ___ Will you take __ my love __ and give

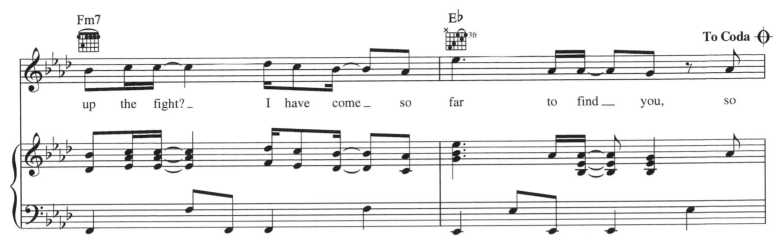

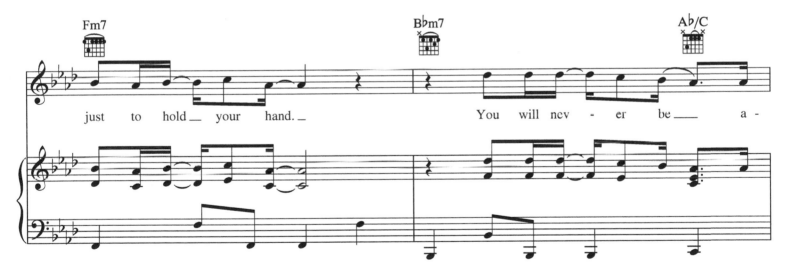

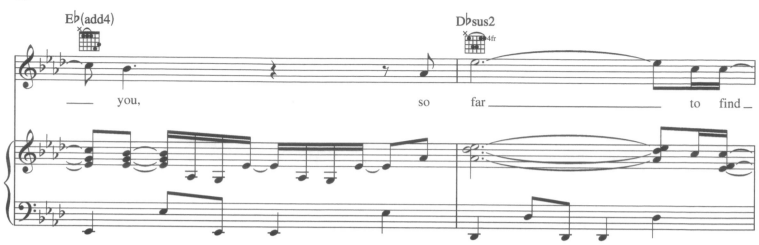

you, so far to find

you. You were fight - ing and

fear - ful, you were hid - ing your heart a - way.

But I was try - ing so hard to show

you, 'cause there were no words that I could say.

If you could see my heart, you would

know that all I want to do is care for you.

D.S. al Coda

far to find you. Here in your eyes, I see re-

flec - tions of __ my - self, __ how I'm the child __ that's real - ly run-

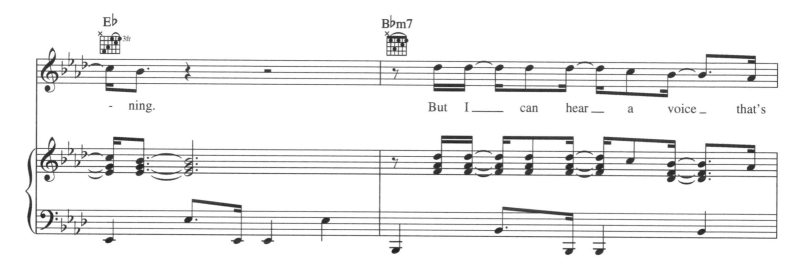

- ning. But I __ can hear __ a voice __ that's

whis - per - ing __ my name, __ say - ing, "Come to Me; __ don't run from Me. __ I'm

all you need, __ and I __ am call - ing. Will you let Me hold __ you in __ My

far to find you. Will you take My love and give

up the fight? I have come so far to find you, so

far to find you. From Heav-en's throne down to a

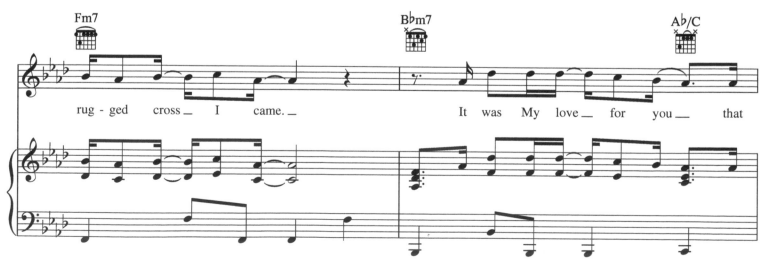

rug-ged cross I came. It was My love for you that

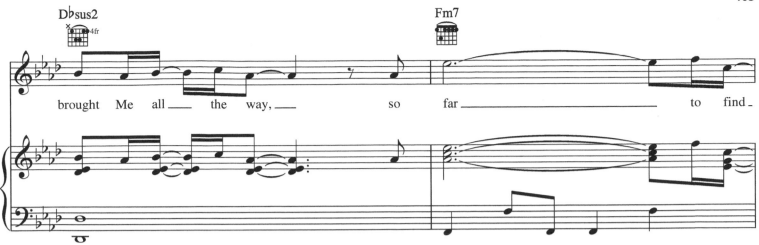

brought Me all ___ the way, ___ so far _____ to find ___

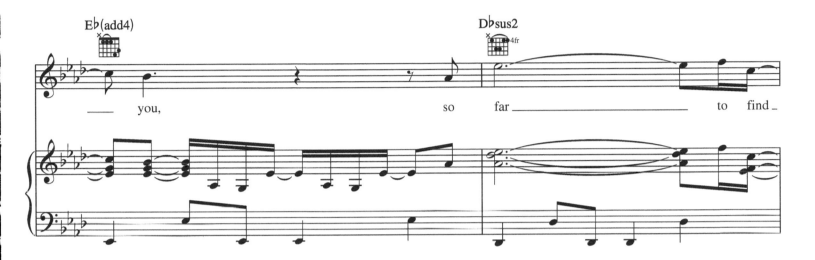

___ you, ___ so far _____ to find ___

___ you. You were bro - ken, ___ a -

ban - doned, ___ and cry - ing ___ all a - lone. ___

CONTEMPORARY
Christian Artist Folios
Arranged for Piano, Voice and Guitar

FROM HAL LEONARD

The Jeremy Camp Collection
00307200 .... $17.99

**Jeremy Camp – We Cry Out:
The Worship Project**
00307178 .... $16.99

**Johnny Cash – My Mother's
Hymn Book**
00306641 .... $17.99

Casting Crowns – Lifesong
00306748 .... $16.95

**Casting Crowns – Come to the
Well**
00307346 .... $16.99

Casting Crowns – Thrive
00125333 .... $16.99

**Casting Crowns – Until the
Whole World Hears**
00307107 .... $16.99

**Casting Crowns – The Very
Next Thing**
00196585 .... $16.99

The Crabb Family Collection
00233193 .... $16.99

**Best of Andrae Crouch –
2nd Edition**
00306017 .... $19.99

**David Crowder*Band –
Give Us Rest**
00307390 .... $16.99

**David Crowder*Band –
Remedy**
08748934 .... $14.95

Lauren Daigle – Look Up Child
00284958 .... $17.99

The Kirk Franklin Collection
00307222 .... $17.99

**The Greatest Songs of Bill &
Gloria Gaither**
00306613 .... $17.99

**Keith & Kristyn Getty –
Awaken the Dawn**
00123655 .... $11.99

**Keith & Kristyn Getty –
In Christ Alone**
00123656 .... $11.99

Amy Grant – Greatest Hits
00306948 .... $17.95

Keith Green – The Greatest Hits
00306981 .... $16.95

**Keith Green – The Ministry
Years, Volume 1**
00306162 .... $19.99

**Keith Green –
The Ultimate Collection**
00306518 .... $19.99

**Steve Green –
The Ultimate Collection**
00306784 .... $22.99

**The Michael Gungor Band –
Ancient Skies**
08751208 .... $19.99

Brandon Heath – What If We
00307151 .... $16.99

**Israel Houghton – Live from
Another Level**
08746591 .... $19.95

**Bishop T.D. Jakes & The
Potter's House Mass Choir –
The Storm Is Over**
00306456 .... $14.95

Kari Jobe – Where I Find You
00307381 .... $17.99

**Days of Elijah – The Best of
Robin Mark**
00306944 .... $16.95

The Best of MercyMe
00118899 .... $19.99

MercyMe – Welcome to the New
00128518 .... $16.99

Bart Millard – Hymned No. 1
08746747 .... $15.95

**Nicole C. Mullen –
The Ultimate Collection**
00307131 .... $17.99

Newsboys – Greatest Hits
00306956 .... $17.95

The Best of Joe Pace
08746468 .... $24.95

Twila Paris – Greatest Hits
00306449 .... $14.95

Sandi Patti Anthology
00490473 .... $24.99

**Elvis Presley -
Songs Of Inspiration**
00308175 .... $17.99

Elvis – Ultimate Gospel
00306988 .... $17.99

The Best of Matt Redman
00307080 .... $16.99

**Matt Redman –
Sing like Never Before:
The Essential Collection**
00116963 .... $19.99

**Matt Redman –
Where Angels Fear to Tread**
08739252 .... $12.95

Switchfoot – The Best Yet
00307030 .... $19.99

**Tenth Avenue North –
Over and Underneath**
00307111 $16.99

**Third Day – Lead Us Back:
Songs of Worship**
00145263 .... $16.99

Third Day – Offerings II
All I Have to Give
00306541 .... $16.95

Third Day – Worship Offerings
Collector's Edition Songbook
08751206 .... $19.95

The Best of TobyMac
00113441 .... $17.99

**Chris Tomlin –
And If Our God Is for Us**
00307187 .... $16.99

Chris Tomlin – Burning Lights
00115644 .... $16.99

**The Chris Tomlin Collection –
2nd Edition**
00306951 .... $17.99

**Chris Tomlin –
How Great Is Our God:
The Essential Collection**
00307362 .... $16.99

Chris Tomlin – Love Ran Red
00139166 .... $16.99

Chris Tomlin – Never Lose Sight
00201955 .... $16.99

The Best of Matthew West
00159489 .... $16.99

The Best of Cece Winans
00306912 .... $16.99

**Darlene Zschech –
Kiss of Heaven**
08739773 .... $16.95

HAL•LEONARD®
For a complete listing of the products we have available,
visit us online at www.halleonard.com

0220
008

Prices, contents, and availability subject to change without notice.